Copyright

All rights reserved. No part of this publication may be reproduced, distributed, or transmitted in any form or by any means, including photocopying, recording, or other electronic or mechanical methods, without the prior written permission of the publisher, except in the case of brief quotations embodied in critical reviews and certain other non-commercial uses permitted by copyright law.

The author retains all rights. No part of this book may be reproduced or transmitted in any form or by any means, electronic or mechanical, including photocopying, recording, or by any information storage and retrieval system without permission in writing from the author except. The unauthorised reproduction, sharing, or distribution of this copyrighted work is illegal.

If you do not have a dream, how can you have a dream come true?

MINDSET IS KEY

Having a strong and resilient mindset will make you more likely to succeed because you will:

- **Be more resilient to stress and setbacks**
- **Acknowledge your weaknesses**
- **Admit what isn't working**
- **Increase your mental resilience and self-confidence**

UNDERSTANDING YOUR WHY

Knowing your Why is one of life's greatest joys. It is to wake up in the morning with a clear sense of purpose. Being clear on your Why can help you:

- **Have strong and clear boundaries**
- **Clear goals, from your dreams and visions**
- **Understand your values**
- **Know what legacy you want to leave behind**

These are the necessary requirements to Create Salon Success.

This can lead to fulfilment and happiness and the Beauty Business of your dreams.

I'M A BEAUTICIAN NOT MAGICIAN

It seems appropriate that the first main chapter is named after the subtitle of the book. You may be wondering why I have chosen this title. I am sure you will agree though. Sometimes we are expected to perform miracles.

We have to be very polite to avoid confrontation but sometimes clients do expect a little, if not a lot, more than we can give. For example a client came to me and said 'you have been recommended by friend, she says you are fantastic at eyebrow shapes'. I do love an eyebrow shape so of course I was flattered.

I was chatting to her during the consultation and she lifted her fringe up and said 'what can you do with these?' I kid you not, there was no eyebrow!!

She had plucked them ALL off.

To be honest I was not sure how to respond. I was 24 back then and thought 'oh my goodness what can I say?' Anyway, I could not hold back.

I simply said 'are you joking?'

She said she kept getting them uneven, so she just carried on and on plucking away. 'You are not kidding' I said.

I laughed (very politely of course) and said 'you are going to have to come back, as I do not have any hair I can stick on haha'. We had a laugh about it and we built a lovely relationship.

Seriously what was I meant to do? I mean, now, I offer 4D eyebrows, I could have done something. But back then things like that did not exist.

Nothing surprises me anymore but that is not to say I cannot be shocked because it still shocks me with what clients think we can do or the expectation that is put on us as Beauty Therapists.

You know when people want nail extensions on when they have not got any nails for them to stick to. That client who is in first thing and wants to swap and cannot comprehend you are fully booked.

The walk-in client who sees you stood at reception and thinks you can fit them in for a treatment and is not happy when you can't.

There are so many examples but they can just make us annoyed, so I would rather make you laugh with funny stories. Like I said **'I'm a beautician not a magician'.**

I know we are Therapists, but it rhymes haha!

MY BELIEFS

My name is Louisa Ashforth and I am a Beauty Therapist of twenty years. I am a Salon Owner and my passion is Holistic Therapies.

Holistic is being aware of external influences, as well as what is going on inside both your mind and body. It is when you are looking at any problem as a 'whole' not just want you can see.
I believe if we take time out of our busy lives and listen to our bodies, they can heal themselves.

Many of us forget to take care of ourselves yet we recommend clients do this all the time. My goal is to inspire Salon Owners to have a Beauty Salon that works for them; helping people Create Salon Success.

Success has a different meaning to many. For me, it is having a work/life balance. Not having to work one hundred hours a week to make a salon work. I help people understand how your mindset is key to Creating Salon Success.

This has taken me a long time to learn and I want to share a little bit about me and my salon experiences.

Being a Holistic Therapist helps me understand the importance of looking at the possible course of a problem, not just what can be seen is a result of the problem. This is the same when we look at what treatments to recommend as well as business, mindset and many other areas of life.

I knew early on in my Beauty career that Holistic Therapy was the path for me and wanted to explore it more. In 2003 I began my journey into Reiki.

I am a Reiki Master, of 18 years, and I live my life by the Reiki Principles and my spiritual beliefs. These Principles are not exclusive to Reiki Practitioners.

I imagine most people can resonate with these ideals, regardless of their spiritual beliefs. They are practical, simple and to be fair they are common sense.

However, like many things, they may be simple but may not always be so easy to implement all the time. They require daily practice and continuous reinforcement.

This can be through daily visualisation, meditation or journaling.

- Just for today I will not worry
- Just for today I will not be angry
- Just for today I will do my work honestly
- Just for today I will give thanks for my many blessings
- Just for today I will be kind to my neighbour and every living thing

Reiki Principles can be applied to everyday living. However, it is not necessary to memorise them or change your Spiritual Beliefs either.

Nevertheless, as a Reiki Practitioner, it is important to be aware of them. Maybe take a moment to think about how these Principles could be applied to your life and allow yourself to feel whether you resonate with them.

I love to incorporate my beliefs into my business and I hope to inspire others too.

The Beauty Industry is extremely fast paced and always moving forward. In my opinion it can be quite brutal; from running a business to the people we have to deal with. It is important to keep up. This can be difficult especially without a support network. By this I mean there is so much competition but we do not have to be in competition with each other, we can support each other instead.

Over the years I have learnt that having a likeminded community helps keep my mindset in check and keep me on track. I have formed this kind of community in the form of a Membership Site: www.CreatingSalonSuccess.co.uk and this helps Salon Owners understand how mindset plays a major part in Creating Salon Success.

I hope you enjoy this book; it is raw and honest but please bear in mind it is a journey of 20 years and it is hard to put into chapters in a book. What I wanted to do was create a book full strategies, education, and funny stories from my experiences along the way. There are so many stories of the crazy goings off in a salon. Of course there are only a few I can include because I respect clients privacy.

I hope to leave you feeling inspired but also give you some tips on ways you could run your business smoothly. Maybe learn from some of my mistakes and help you create a work/life balance and achieve Salon Success. Something that is difficult in any business, but especially Beauty.

I wanted to write this book 10 years ago. I told a friend I wanted to tell people Beauty Therapy is not all the glamour it seems on the outside. It is blinking hard work. They just said they are 10 a penny and there is no money in it. I understood what he meant. However, I realise now I am not doing this for the money.

I am not trying to be the next number 1 selling book. How cool would that be though!? I want to share experiences. I want to tell people a real account of salon life and business, well mine anyway.

My clients are always saying we should have a fly on the wall documentary. If ever I came to work with a little more makeup than usual clients would always ask 'have you got a camera on us?'. I wish I had a camera sometimes as my salon has always had, and still does have good fun vibes.

Fun times have been had in my salon with clients and staff!! Most of the fun times, I have to say, is when my Mum began to join the team on a more permanent basis. She was meant to stop work but she comes in the salon and we just have so much fun. Clients love her!

Anyway, I digress. Be prewarned I will do that a lot. What is that saying, 'sorry, not sorry.' There is no point as I cannot say it will change. Those who know me know how true that is! Haha.

Yes, this book has taken me some time, but eventually it is here. I decided to do it anyway, despite opinions from others and maybe back then I would not have been so open and honest. Not because I was not honest, I just was still in a place where I was hiding myself. I was so much better, do not get me wrong. But it has taken me a while to really put myself out there and allow people to see me flaws and all.

There may be a lot of these kind of books. I wanted mine to be a little different by including some stories from clients. I do not want to be rude or disrespectful to clients but these need to be shared.

People always ask if I have any stories. I generally say no, however if I do share any, they will be the ones in this book. The stories are much funnier when I act them out for you, but you will have to use some of your imagination too.

I respect my clients and what they share with me. They are my friends and I share with them too. Imagine what they have on me!! I think it is always wise to always keep confidentiality.

We pride ourselves on that in our salon. However, once a client had split from her partner and one of my staff knew about it. It was not a nice break up. Not that any are, but you know what I am saying. So, rightly so, my staff member did not share this with me. The next time I was doing the clients' facial, I was chatting away and in true Louisa style I put my foot in it.

I remember she had hurt her arm or something (it is literally 15 years ago) and I said 'ooh you will have to get (I will just call him Greg) to wash your hair'. I was laughing and she was and then she just said 'Louisa, you do know Greg and I are no longer together, don't you?'

Well, obviously I did not otherwise I would not have been banging on about him!

I was thinking 'seriously Louisa!!!'. But she was fine and of course it was not anyone's fault and at least the client knew there was no gossiping about her. May be on that occasion I could have had a heads up.

But hey, all is good!

All the stories in this book are true, even if some feel farfetched. I hope you enjoy learning a bit about me and my journey both in business and spiritually and I hope it gives you some guidance and inspiration for your business too.

Enjoy the read and as always, I hope you get so much value too.

Love and light.
Louisa xx

THOSE PESKY VOICES OF DOUBT

This book has been on my list of goals for some time. Yet fear has been in my way too many times. 'How can I write a book?' 'People like me do not write books.' 'How would I get it published? It will be too expensive'.

It was that ever so familiar voice in my head. That one that is saying 'you are not good enough' or 'what will people think?' People will think 'who does she think she is?'

I was worried of people's judgment and I am sure this is true throughout my many years of business. I guess it was that fear of failure.

Sooooo many voices. Why do we do this? Why do I let the voice of others get inside my head? They are not living my life. I do not judge them, so why do I think they are judging me?

Do you ever think 'why do so many people have an opinion of each other and how they should live?' But we are not all the same, are we?

I can tell you if I had not let voices (mine included) get inside my head, I would have been ahead much faster. However, I am a big believer in 'everything happens for a reason'. Everything comes at the right time!

Cliché I know, but it is my belief. Have you heard of the law of attraction? Something we all are part of, but we may not realise. It is not until you learn about it that you realise how powerful it is and in turn how powerful you can be too. I will talk more about this later.

I believe we all have an amazing gut instinct. However, sometimes those voices take over and we can be too much in our head. This is when we let our head rule our heart. Those voices become so loud we do not listen to our heart.

Maybe, we just cannot hear it anymore. It can become confusing and feel overwhelming. Take a moment, now, and put your hand on your heart and close your eyes. Take three deep breaths in and out. Concentrate on those breaths and centre yourself.

I started my business back when I was 21. I look back at things I would have told my 21-year-old self and I want to share some of these things with you.

Maybe you can relate?

Or maybe some of these things will help to ensure you do not take the same path as me and you can trust in yourself.

The intention of this book is to inspire you to learn from some of my stories and maybe laugh at some too. I want to help you Create Salon Success and have the business you dream of.

I want you to recognise that having a strong, positive mindset and understanding why we do what we do are the key to achieving that successful salon you desire.

I believe we can choose to keep smiling through whatever poop we are going through. Nobody wants to see a miserable face, do they? It is not always easy in our job, is it? But let's get that mask on and smile, right?

You may be thinking what is she talking about? Well, I believe in Beauty we wear a kind of mask (not the COVID ones, haha). Greet your client with a smile and both yours and their worries can fade away, even just for a little while.

How precious is it, that we can create an environment to ease people's worries, even if it is just for the short space of their treatment time?

Just because I speak about wearing a mask, this does not mean we are two faced!

Beauty Therapy jobs are all about putting on a show for people. Not fake - you are authentically you. However, you are creating a place of safety for your clients, no matter what you are going through.

In my opinion, we are a very special breed of people. Yes, advantage can be taken, and therefore we must find ways of handling ourselves in these situations.

To create your dream business it is important to have the following things:

- A strong and positive Mindset
- Understand your 'Why'
- Know your Values
- Create solid boundaries
- Recognise your Dreams and Visions
- Set Goals and Plans
- Trust your gut instincts
- Appreciate you are allowed to say 'No'

Welcome to the world of Louisa; just a snippet of entertainment for you to enjoy and be inspired to 'Create Salon Success' for you.

WORKING IN THE BEAUTY INDUSTRY

Have you always thought you would love to work in the Beauty Industry? Let me share a few things about Beauty as a job or a business.

For me, it is not the high-profile Beauty person to the stars or the celebrity world, that many may think it is. Do not get me wrong, it could be. However, at my salon it is a regular Beauty Therapy job. My salon is gorgeous, a place of tranquillity. However, I always say it is the least glamorous job going and not what people have in mind. More like glorified cleaners, as most of our job is cleaning up!!

I thought I would talk about some of my own experiences in the salon, on a day-to-day basis. I will also go into some of the running of the salon and the fun that can be involved there!

This book is for people who want to get into business in the Beauty Industry or who are perhaps considering a job in Beauty Therapy, or if you already work in the Industry and have just lost your way! I thought it may be helpful to share a few tips with you to help things run a little more smoothly.

Finding a job or being in business in the Beauty world can be tough. Maybe there are no jobs, or maybe there are, but they want someone with a little more experience. I get the frustration. It is a good idea to try to get some work experience in a local salon.

Why not get in touch with one? Be prepared for it to be unpaid, though. However, I know if someone offered me a few hours help in the salon, it would go a long way for when I was looking for staff.

I believe making that sacrifice to work unpaid, could be the fastest way to gain an actual job. Find a way, it may just be worth it. Even if your goal is to start your business, gaining some inside knowledge can be priceless.

I gained experience in a salon just by watching and making tea. I contacted the salon directly. I had to work for free, I did not get a job, but it gave me loads of experience, which I am grateful for. I believe this helped me start my business too, as I really learnt a lot.

The main thing is to not give up! If you are really struggling, perhaps consider setting up a Beauty room at home, or a mobile Beauty business to help you gain more experience and confidence in the industry. Do not forget if you are going to do this, you will need to register as self-employed and organise your own insurance. However, this is a topic for another day.

Take it from me, no two Beauty jobs are the same. That is one of the great things about Beauty Therapy is, it is a very versatile career. It is a great qualification to have, you can have a job working for big named Beauty brands on counters, you can work in a salon, or even set up at home or mobile and want to work hours that suit you. If you are setting up a business, though, please take some notes from this book.   Being around likeminded people and having the right advice is crucial. Consider joining a coaching program, for example like the one I have running on www.CreatingSalonSuccess.co.uk

In Beauty there are so many treatments and it is good to find your passion and focus on it. You may find you have a favourite and want to specialise, working as a nail tech, for example, or perhaps becoming a skincare specialist or masseuse.

Make yourself an expert in that area. Too many of us become a 'Jack of all trades.' I know I did, which just made it difficult when I wanted to concentrate on my passion of skincare and well-being treatments.

The only way to find out what you love is to test the water. Sometimes the thing you expect to love just is not for you. Do not fear change. Work out your purpose and what it is you love to do and what can earn you money.

Understanding why you do what you do, knowing your values and what you want out of life, as well as making sure your pricing is right are crucial points to consider when setting up on your own. If the idea is to work the hours that suit your lifestyle, be strict from the start.

More of these points will be covered throughout this book along with many stories. I am sure you will pick the best and worst bits out, whilst hopefully laughing at some of my escapades.

Like any job, there are good things and bad things about being a Beauty Therapist and being in business. If you are hoping for a super glam job where you just sit and make people look pretty all day, you may be disappointed.

Some days, you might spend your whole day painting nails, perfecting brows and spraying tans. However, other days, you may spend your entire time waxing unmentionable parts of the body, doing a hardcore massage that makes you feel as though you have done an insanity workout. Not to mention those days when you are filing thick dead skin from the bottom of a client's feet.

Dealing with clients can be the best and worst thing about the job. Clients make our business and our day run smoothly. But of course, there is always the odd one or two that do not make your day easier, or pleasant.

Then there is all the cleaning! Like I said, we are like glorified cleaners. Be proud of where you work. Nothing I say is a negative, it is just very honest. You may spend a lot of time during the first few months of your career standing around, answering phones and making tea. These are ways to build customer relationships.

Go and deliver leaflets, chat to people in their gardens, make yourself known. These are extremely important parts of the role. In Beauty, customer relations are more key than you can imagine. It is the small things, that go a long way. For example, clients love to be greeted by their name.

I always remember in a tanning shop I rented space in; you will find out more about this soon. I greeted a client by her name, and she said, 'Oh it is so nice when someone remembers your name.'

I thought this was strange, but it turned out she stopped going to her previous salon because they did not remember her. This made her feel like rubbish and not someone of value.

So, it just shows you, doesn't it? Doing ordinary things and doing them well.

Our job is somewhat simple, really. Customers just want to feel like we care. Is that not human nature in general? We all want to feel valued and cared about.

Beauty is not hard; I just think it takes a very special individual. That is you, by the way!

Have you heard of Maslow's Hierarchy of needs? If not, it is a theory of what motivates humans to do things. By this I mean, what is motivating them to come back to your salon or back to you as a therapist.

The way I take it when it comes to our job is, when someone feels their physiological needs are met, they will be happy; we offer them drinks and are hospitable.

When they psychological needs are met; they feel safe in their environment (your salon), they have a relationship with you and their self-esteem is raised, because you make them feel good.

They feel love and like they belong somewhere. This is important to clients; to be made to feel welcome. We create those interpersonal relationships with them such as trust and acceptance.

They are then fulfilled, which of course is the ultimate goal for anyone. This is down to the way you treat them as a customer.

I hope you can begin to see the way we treat a customer and how we make them feel is crucial to any Therapist and any Beauty Business.

FULFILMENT

I speak briefly about the needs of our clients. However, the feeling of being valued and fulfilled is not only for your clients this is also for you as a Business Owner.

Your needs must be fulfilled too. This is why we should be aware of what we need to feel fulfilled as an individual to have a successful business.

Measuring success is not always about salary and job titles. Personally, for me, success means more of a balanced life. The title and salary are a very small part.

Of course money always helps, but to me success is more about happiness. Not externally, internally.

I am more interested in having a balance of my mental health, physical health, free time and of course enjoying what I do.

I could earn a massive amount of money, but without the other elements I would not feel fulfilled or satisfied by my life.

Tony Robbin's adapted Maslow's theory and created a quiz. Why don't you have a look at this quiz and discover which human need is driving your behaviours.

I took this quiz, and my driving force is: Uncertainty. I would never have guessed this.

However, these are the strengths according to the results:

- **A sense of adventure:** You're willing to roll up your sleeves and try something new, from food to employment. Others might see the unknown as scary, but for you it's life.
- **Adaptability**: You interact with all kinds of people in all kinds of places. You can change and enjoy doing so.
- **Many interests:** What are you not interested in? You can make stimulating conversation about almost any topic. If you don't already know something, you're eager to learn.
- **Energy:** Your move around, physically and mentally. You avoid habits and routines that could make you bored.

I can relate to these areas, and I would say it is pretty accurate. There are clearly areas I need to work on here.

It is always good to analyse what makes you 'tick', however we must be open to adaption as well.

According to the results, here are some of the negative sides:

- **Plan averse:** Always thinking things will change can lead to an unwillingness to plan in jobs, investments or relationships; limiting possible new experiences in the future.
- **Learned helplessness:** It's easy to fall into the trap of thinking you have no control over a situation and just give up, go on to the next thing.

- **Unfocused:** You can get involved with too many things and become careless about yourself. When something is not interesting, you're likely to drop it, even if you'll reap rewards later on.
- **Addictive or destructive behaviours:** Your need for ever-changing stimulation may lead to developing patterns that make you feel certain you will get that variety. This can manifest in various forms, like over/under-eating, drinking or drug abuse.

I do not see these as negatives and I am aware of my behaviours, which is key to success. Of course, this is my opinion. We all have traits that can be seen as a negative to others.

These points could almost indicate I could be unreliable. However, it may look that way, but I am one of the most reliable people ever. Almost to my own detriment.

That is not to say I never let people down. However, reliability in myself and others is a trait I value highly. Unreliability is one of my biggest 'bug bears' about people.

This is why I keep my circle small. I have many acquaintances, but not many people are in my friendship circle.

The sections above are establishing our basic human needs. Our needs should be remembered all throughout building your business, including from the very start. If we start well, the journey can be so much easier.

Why not take the quiz? I found it interesting. We all have the same basic needs; yet we can all place higher importance in different areas.

If you are struggling to see where you place more importance, it may be worth taking the quiz.

Clarifying your own human needs can help you discover your life's direction and how you can create fulfilment.

www.core.tonyrobbins.com/driving-force-6/

'THAT'S WHAT YOU DO WHEN YOU ARE SELF-EMPLOYED'

If I had a pound for every time, I have heard this line, 'That's what you do when you are self-employed'. Believe me, I would not need a Beauty Salon, as I would already be a millionaire!

It always comes from someone who has never been self-employed in their life.

Throughout this book I am going to talk about some mistakes I have made during my business, some funny stories (I hope) and offer some strategies that you could implement to help you avoid the same mistakes that I did.

One of the first mistakes I want to mention, is not following your gut instincts. I believe we all have gut instincts, and if we listened to them, we would get much further, in a shorter time. However, instead, we often ignore these instincts. This can be when we let our head rule our heart. It is when we let those voices in our head become so loud it is all we can hear. This can be your own voice, often fear speaking, or it can be the voice of others.

Usually, these people have your best interests at heart, but have never been self-employed in their lives. Do you ever find you listen to others, maybe people older and who you consider wiser than you? Although, you are the one who knows your business.

The first piece of advice

Only take business advice from someone who has been there and done it.

Someone who can evidence it too. The reason being is people often think they know, but how can they? They are possibly not even a Beauty Therapist; I know those giving me advice were not. I would often be unable to speak when I had finished work, through exhaustion more than anything. I was working 12-hour days, charging ridiculously cheap prices, and generally not enjoying anything at all, especially not my business.

However, I had made my bed I had to lie in it. I had my own business and I had left my job, so suck it up! That was very much my attitude, because I was told that is what you do when you are self-employed.

I was 21 and I had been travelling the world, until now. I was used to going out and living life to the max. I could not do this with my business, because I was 21 and, absolutely, exhausted. This was a massive adjustment for me.

Now, I was working 7 days a week and 12 hour days. Any time I complained or said I cannot do this, people just responded saying: 'that's what you do when you are self-employed'. If I could tell my 21 year old self anything it would be:

'It does not have to be that way. No, it is not what you have to do when you are self-employed and is definitely not the best strategy for setting up a successful and sustainable business.'

But I knew no different, so I was like 'oh ok then. Shut up moaning Louisa!'.

Oh, how I wish I had a me, the now me that is, back then. I would have been so successful, so much more quickly.

When you believe you can do it alone and you do not need a coach/mentor, believe me it is so much better to have one. It makes life and business so much easier.

You don't know what you don't know and there is no shame in that. But it is about getting the right advice from the right people. I had no idea what a mentor was, nor did I know I could have one, let alone need one.

Of course, costs need to be kept low. However, if we all could set up our businesses correctly, from the beginning, it would be so much easier. Plus, mentors do not have to be expensive. It is one of the reasons why I developed Creating Salon Success (www.CreatingSaloinSuccess.co.uk).

I believe, so many people get to that point in business where they no longer want to do it. It is too hard; you have no life and very soon resentment kicks in. It did for me anyway.

Now, everything was going well for me, money was coming in, but I was absolutely shattered. I was so unhappy and very stressed and to be honest I think I started to hate what I had created. I struggled to cope, and I had no idea what to do. So, I just kept going. I do not know how.

I had, and still do have an amazing relationship with my clients and I think this is what has kept me going, somehow. I do not think any of them knew how I felt as I kept it from everyone and almost felt like I had this secret life.

One life where I was this fantastic Business Owner, looking really successful and the other where I was crying at night. Not just at night actually, I often cried throughout the day too. Especially if a client did not show up for an appointment. I took it so personally.

No shows mean no money, which means no income for me and how was I meant to live? It just confirmed to me that nobody cared.

Crying myself to sleep and crying over no shows is something I actually felt ashamed of, rightly or wrongly. I am a strong character and I felt, once again, people would judge me and believed that I could not cope. Truth be told I couldn't, but I did not realise it yet.

Do not ask me how I got up every day and went into my salon as I cannot tell you how I did this. Looking back, I think I was really depressed and extremely stressed, but I was the master at hiding it. To be truthful, I had some very unhealthy coping mechanisms. One of them was turning my back on so many people, including family.

I was struggling so much I just did not want anyone to see me, but somehow, I went to work, because I had made a commitment and I could not let people down. This mattered so much to me. I could find this autopilot, which helped me hide my pain inside and get on. It was like I was another person at work, like an actor on stage. I am in no way a fake person, but I started to feel like a fake and a phoney. Believe me this did nothing for my self-esteem and self-worth. I hate liars and I felt like I was becoming the ultimate liar. I hid myself away from everyone and put on a front. It was still me, do not get me wrong. Nobody wanted to hear about my sadness and depression, did they? And I could not let people down.

Now, I have learnt that sometimes we must let people down to look after ourselves. This is NOT wrong.

If I ever said anything, all I heard back was 'that is what you do when you are self-employed' or 'the joys of running your own business'. This just made me think, well why can't I do it? Why am I struggling soooo much? I am a failure, I am rubbish, I am not good enough.

Even typing this I take myself back to the pain I felt. I am sat here struggling to see the screen because of the tears in my eyes. I am so sad for this person. This person is so unrecognisable to me now and my heart breaks thinking I or anyone could ever feel this way. I was very unaware of all of this because it just crept up on me.

All I remember is arguing with so many people, family members. Especially my Mum. Those who know me and her know how close we are and probably cannot imagine us being this way.

My Mum comes everywhere with me and helps with the skincare and salon, she is totally my right-hand man. But back then she could not help me either. She kept telling me to go and get help and I remember screaming 'you just don't understand'. No, she did not and how could she? I did not even understand how I was feeling myself.

I started rapidly losing weight. I have never been fat, but I was 6 and a half stone. I shopped at new look kids' section, which sounds great, but it really was not. In true Louisa style I would often joke about how many clothes I could buy for such a small amount of money.

I started with awful acne, which used to wake me up in the night it was so painful.

My Mum then thought I had an eating disorder because I would spend so long in the toilet and as soon as I had eaten whatever was in me seemed to want to come out. Not being too graphic, let's call it a number 2.

This happened every time I ate, and I mean **every** time! This was certainly not a fun time for me. I brush over the subject with ease, but it was awful. Especially when I started dating my, now, husband.

I often sent him home after he had taken me for a lovely meal, or I had to leave his house. His Mum thought I was a little weird. To be fair I do not blame her. It was no fun!

The aches I got in my stomach were immense. I had to spend ages just sat on the toilet. Sometimes, I could not go to the toilet, but I could not leave the toilet either. I could be there hours, sometimes. This led to bruises on my knees from resting my elbows on them for so long. Obviously because I was just sat on the toilet waiting for my body to do whatever it needed to do.

I will leave that subject now. However, just for the record I did not have an eating disorder, but this once again caused arguments between my Mum and me. She was trying to help in the way she knew how. She was not helping she just did not get it. That is what I thought, anyway.

Time went on. Maybe 3 years passed and it turned out I had IBS caused by stress. Because food would not stay in my body, my body was not absorbing any nutrients, which then led to acne. I just felt a mess!!

So mentally I was unhappy, physically I was unhappy, job wise I was unhappy, friendships had dwindled because I was not open, I felt family hated me and I worked too much. So, in my world nobody cared about me.

As long as people got their treatments done people were happy. I just felt that nobody cared about me. I felt I was just here for everyone else's benefit.

There were so many times I did not see the point in life. Quite sad, I know.

I am being totally vulnerable and open here, which again is something I struggle with. I am sharing because if you ever feel resentment, stress, feeling like you have no friends, nobody cares, financial worries, busy but no profit and so many other things I have mentioned please know you are not alone.

When it comes to any business, mindset is everything.

This leads me to...

The second piece of advice

And probably THE most important piece too.

'Look after your mental health'.

Unknowingly to me I think a big turning point here was learning Reiki 1.

My Mum signed us up for the course. See, she was here again helping me! I did not realise at the time, because do not forget she did not understand (I thought anyway).

At first, I thought my Reiki Master was bonkers. The whole thing was bonkers and I had an attitude that, to be frank, stunk! Of course, I kept my attitude in. I had only come on the course to be nice to my Mum and do something with her.

Funny, isn't it? This massively helped me and I still use it today. It is becoming more and more popular nowadays. This is something I was unknowingly grateful for at the time and so much more grateful for now.

Reiki helps you become very aware of the inner you and how you feel. Trusting your instincts. I am not saying I am perfect at it, but without Reiki I wonder where I would have been. It is completely life changing!

In case you wondered, I carried on with Reiki for 3 years and became a Reiki Master. When I walked in the room to do my Masters. Gerald, my Reiki Master, said to me:

'You are a different person from the first day you stepped in this room'.

Of course, it was a bit of a roll my eyes moment (so rude, I know). But you know something that statement and time is very special to me. Inside I rolled my eyes, I think, because I was embarrassed. But how right was he? I really was a different person.

I had started to put things in place to work on my mindset. Gosh, if I had started it all so much sooner... I say that a lot. But I know it is all about divine timing. I say it because if you can relate to anything I say, do not hesitate to get help. Whether it be reading self-development books or finding that (been there and done that) mentor.

This is from the start of your business, not when you get to the point where I was at, and this is why I say set your business up to be sustainable.

I am ending this chapter here as it is not meant to be doom and gloom, but business is not always a happy place, but it can be! Please get that mentor/coach as soon as you can.

Always the over talker, just one more thing.

Before I started even understanding mindset and 'working on it'. I had some therapy. Talking it out with a professional. Once again this was not easy. I tried the doctors, that did not work for me. I tried hypnotherapy and this was brilliant, however the person moved away.

It is all about finding the 'right' person for you and I did find the right person. I have had a few and I did not change because it wasn't right. I had just got what I needed at that time. Our mental health, like the Beauty Industry, is always changing and we need to be aware of what is happening to us. This is why self-care is so important and why I will speak about mindset all the time. Because without a strong mindset we can feel like we are losing control of our own lives.

I always felt people would judge me if they knew I struggled. I still do and that is why I still have a Therapist.

There is no shame. Business (and life) can be challenging and learning how to deal with these challenges are what can and will move us forward.

Surround yourself with like minded people!

Be part of a community.

Break that stigma regarding mental health.

Please do not feel all 'woe is me'. Take positive action and speak to someone. Friends and family are great, but they are not qualified to deal with any problems. Yes they can lend an ear and that is lovely. But sometimes we need some 'real' help.

The kind that will help us make the changes you need to move you forward in life and business.

Do not feel ashamed or think of yourself as a failure, like I did. There is help out there and you have a life to lead and your dream business to run. Make it happen!! You can do this!!

SPRAY TANS

Wow the emotional roller coaster I feel I have just been on writing that last chapter, I promised some funny's and I think we need one here.

Let me start with spray tans…

I am sure you have many of your own stories, but I just thought I would share a few of mine.

Spray tans are very intimate. Why? Well, the client is nearly naked!!

As a therapist, we generally do not even notice as we are too busy making sure all the body is covered, evenly.

So, they do not phase me at all.

However, on occasion, even I can be thrown.

I am no prude and bodies do not bother me. But when you walk in, and a client does not pre warn you they are getting fully naked. You cannot help being like… ooh ok!

And yes, I mean naked, completely naked.

This is all well and good, until you are spraying your client and you have to bob down to spray their legs…

Before you know it you are head-to-head with an area you did not plan for!

Slight awkward feeling, but hey we are all the same.

It is no problem on my behalf, just sometimes nice to be prewarned!!! It is just a little story that makes me chuckle. Especially when the client says:

'I would not get naked for anyone else but you'

Why thank you most kind!! It is flattering really. As the client was meaning she was so comfortable with me that she did not want any strap marks whatsoever and no knickers meant no straps at all! After all is that not the point of a spray tan?

Do you feel embarrassed?

A client once asked me if I was embarrassed doing spray tans?

I said no not at all, although, if I did ever feel slightly awkward it would have to be when I have to ask clients to lift their boobs up. Big or small, you know those half-moons you can get?

She replied 'it is not my boobs you have to worry about it is under bum cheeks'.

As she did this, she spun round bent over and lifted her bum. We both fell about laughing. Obviously, this would be way funnier if you knew the client and I had that fly on the wall documentary!! She may not agree, but it is one of my favourite stories. Clients can make us feel so special. You may be wondering how this situation makes me feel special.

It is the way clients feel around us.

For someone to feel that comfortable around me and the relationship we have built, is so special. Often it is this relationship that stops us giving up, when you feel like 'I cannot do this anymore.' You know that feeling?

Men and spray tans

Sometimes I am never sure if people just try and get a reaction.

I do not want to label all men the same, so please do not think I am ever saying that. However, often some of my funny stories are about men.

I have plenty of my lovely clients, but the most entertaining and craziest, often are to do with men. I never want to share personal stories about my clients.

However, if it feels people are trying to get a reaction, I want to share these.

I once had this guy in the salon, who needed to have a naked spray tan. Like I said I am ok with naked bodies. It did feel a little like they wanted to show off, though. However, they did come back for a few. So, maybe it was genuine. But the other side of the argument could be when they did not get a reaction, they stopped coming in. Who knows…??

The only slightly embarrassing thing here, was I did not quite plan for having to ask them to move their willy from side to side in order for me to spray where I needed.

Again, when I had to bob down, I was far too close to an area than I would have liked. So, it was slightly awkward, but it is fine. I found it all more amusing than anything. Definitely memorable though!!

Lesson – Manage expectations, both yours and your clients. Maybe have some questions you ask or instructions you want to give before booking in a spray tan. No problem telling them to scrub, no moisturiser or deodorant. Maybe incorporate other discussions into this too.

Such as: 'Please note we do not offer naked spray tans, paper pants are provided.'

It all comes back to the consultation with clients, doesn't it?

FRUSTRATION

Are you happy within your business? I often see posts in forums or Facebook groups saying if they had their time again, they would keep their money and not start a Beauty business. I totally get that; but I also find it quite sad.

When you invest so much time and effort into something, it is almost soul destroying to think it is not providing you with job satisfaction, fulfilment, or giving you a balanced life.

Ask yourself these questions:

> Do you ever feel frustrated with your business?
>
> Do you resent it a little because it feels like one crisis after another?
>
> Do you wish you could give it all up?
>
> Does it provide you with a healthy income for yourself?
>
> Do you have a profit for the business?
>
> Do you feel negative or positive about your business?
>
> Do you have a plan of where you want to be with your business in 12 months or more?

The negative answers to these questions are very familiar to me and this leads to frustration.

I remember when frustration was the primary feeling I had when thinking about my Beauty salon.

I continually thought about what I did not want and did not like about my business.

We all know, we attract what we focus on. Of course, the more I dwelled on problems, the more problems I found.

My business started to feel more like a noose around my neck than this amazing place I had envisaged.

I had always loved travelling and I felt my business stopped me from doing things I loved. I felt very stuck and lost enjoyment in business and life. We can become consumed by our businesses, I get that and it is not a bad thing. We just could do with choosing a better balance.

After all, everything does come down to a choice and quite often we can feel like we do not have a choice. This in itself is something we are choosing to believe. If we had strategies we could use or felt like someone really does understand and can offer advice or help we could make the changes for a healthier mind and business.

Do not forget, you created the business. It is not a monster out to get you.

We often allow things to happen to us and we accept things, but then they become a way of life. For so long we can cope and handle it, but then it can easily get on top of us, and it is not so easy to manage.

Feelings of resentment and frustration affect us in ways that diminish us.

These negative feelings reduce our capacity for problem-solving and it is these feelings that can prevent us achieving the results we want.

The funny thing is when we feel frustration, it is only us that know. Our business doesn't and nor do those around us.

Do you ever feel like screaming at people?

'You just do not understand!'

As you can tell, I thought this a lot. Can you relate?

You are the only person feeling the physical effects of your frustration!

The good news is feelings are caused by our thoughts and we can decide what we want to think.

Which means we can decide how we want to feel. How do you want to feel about your business? Do you want to love it again?

I make it sound simple, but if you want to love it, then love it.

List all the things you thought your business would give you. Do not think, yes but it doesn't give me those things. Change your perspective.

'Decide on purpose to love your business again.'

Your business is like any other relationship, it takes work and nourishment. If you put in stress, frustration and even blame that is what you will get back.

Your business reflects how you feel. Do not forget we are powerful, and we can make things happen through law of attraction.

Did your mum ever say?

'Be careful what you wish for'

I will talk more about the Law of Attraction later.

When we begin looking at our thoughts objectively, we can see that resentment is not just a waste of time, it's illogical.

It is our business. We own it and can decide how we feel about it.

More often, than not, we are the ones responsible for creating the situations we perceive as a trap because our identity is wrapped up in the business. When something goes wrong, do you make it mean something about you?

I know I did. This led me to overwork and overmanage. Burn out will hit and this way cannot continue long term. We can make our business work for us.

When these feelings kick in gather perspective and stay focused on your goals by asking yourself:

> Why am I choosing to feel this way?
>
> What am I making this mean?
>
> What else could this mean?
>
> What am I learning and how can it help me?

Business does not have be this hard and nor should it be. But who teaches you to run a business? Nobody, right?

I believe it should be taught in college; however, I guess that is why there are people like me around.

Frustration feelings are genuine even though some business problems may not be as terrible as they initially feel.
But I get the feelings are not nice and if we can choose ways to help us feel better, it would be so much nicer.

Do you agree?

Business is not always a bed of roses, but it truly can give us an amazing life.

THE PERSON BEHIND THE LA BRAND

I know I have already got quite deep and you can tell business is something I can get very emotional about. This is because I understand how difficult it is and if I can help you avoid some of the mistakes I made, I will be happy.

I want to share with you some things that have really helped me become successful. Things I had no idea about or did not think would benefit me. Oh, how wrong I was and maybe if I had learnt about them and implemented them far sooner, believe me, I would be so much further on.

Maybe I would already be in my dream house in Australia by the beach. To be more specific Palm Beach, you know where Home and Away is filmed? Anyway, I digress…

So, let me tell you a little more about me and my business and where it all began.

You could call me a Beauty Entrepreneur, which feels strange, yes, but I am and I am guessing you are too, right?

My name is Louisa Ashforth, I am 41 years old, from Aston in Sheffield, UK. I am someone who, since being able to, has always had a part time job, alongside school and clearly was never afraid of hard work.

I left school at 16, not staying on for A levels due to me not really knowing what I wanted to do.

Beauty Therapy was never on the agenda. I would never really have classed myself as a girly girl. Plus Beauty Therapy was not a big thing back in 1996.

The only course available was hairdressing, however the stereotype existed that you only did hair if you weren't very bright.

Now, do not get me wrong, I never thought this. I remember telling my careers advisor I wanted to go into travel. I had always had a passion for travelling and dreamed of travelling the world, whilst working. The careers advisor said 'people like you do not go into travel.' It was kind of a compliment. He was saying I was too clever for travel. I did not take it as a compliment as I just wanted to travel and work in travel.

Hair and Beauty are also classed as non-academic. This is a huge misconception. We all know what is involved in Beauty Therapy. I am sure many of you reading this will be in the industry and screaming at these sentences. It is blinking hard work and that is just to qualify!

The anatomy and physiology are immense, right?

But it is amusing when I tell people I am a Beauty Therapist and I see a person's face look a little unimpressed. I rarely tell people I own my own business as I do not feel the need to impress anyone.

This is in no way me not wanting to. I just really do not like how people make instant judgements. But I guess we can all do that from time to time.

You may think this is slight paranoia on my part, yet when they find out I am in business their whole attitude changes.

I think it takes me back to the careers guy at school. I get it. However, I do not think I would be living the life I have, on the wage I am earning in any employed position.

Anyway, I always thought I would be a lawyer or something like that. But I could never defend someone I thought was guilty. Or what if I got the wrong person sent to prison. Of course there are more sides to law but that is what I thought back then.

I decided to carry on at a place I had been working at a weekend, whilst at school. This was an admin job in a sales office, at a timber supplier. They offered me full time after I had finished school.

My Mum and Dad had brought me up with the statement 'If you want to leave school, you go and get a job, you are not sponging from us.' It sounds harsh, doesn't it?

I agree with this statement so it does not offend me. Of course, I took the job. I wanted to leave school. Everything just seemed to fall into place.

This was one of the best jobs I have ever had.

I gained so many skills here. Sales, accounts, dealing with customers. These customers were from all walks of life but mainly builders. I had to have broad shoulders working there as the customers did not hold back with what they wanted to say.

Teamwork was paramount too. I worked with another girl in the sales office who was my superior and I am still friends with her to this day.

We had such a good working relationship and we loved having the office to ourselves. So much so, we struggled to get other staff for a while. Not because it was not a good job but because we liked it being the two of us. That is a bit of a secret.

But we quickly realised we had to let others join as we needed help. I also worked with the lads on the yard too who had to shout customer orders through to us. We had to be fast here making sure we had the order correct and charging the right amount.

Funnily enough one of these lads ended up being my husband. He still is in case you were wondering. Although this did not happen for many years after. He came back into my life at THE most perfect time. My life completely changed because of him and I will be forever grateful.

So much was expected of us in this job and these skills have helped me in running my business, so much.

I always craved more out of life, I did not want to settle down and buy a house and stay in the same job forever. I guess I have always been a dreamer.

After a year, of leaving school and doing this job. I was a little bored, only because I always crave more. Not because things were not good.

Opportunities came my way and I have always grabbed as many opportunities as I can. Why not? You never know where it may lead.

For example, myself and a friend were planning on a girly holiday. We were a bit too young, as I was still only 16. This led us to be going over to see my friend's Aunty in Jersey, in the Channel Islands.

In true Louisa style we did not go for a week.

I ended up quitting my job and we got summer jobs over there. I did not come back for 5 years.

CASUALTIES

Building a business is by no means an easy task. If any of you have done this or doing this. Wow!!!

And a massive well done. This is in no way patronising. I genuinely do not think people realise the amount of work and the amount of sacrifices you will make. I know I didn't!

Many self-employed people think I am good at what I do, so I may as well work for myself and have all the money instead of making someone else all the money. Right?

Did you also think, well I can work when I want, do what I want and not answer to anyone?

I am thinking by now you have the same realisation as me and understand it is not quite as simple as that is it?

I have titled this chapter 'casualties.' Maybe to grab your attention, I am not sure to be honest. It just seemed to fit.

Of course, I am not talking about fatal injuries here. I am talking about relationships; romantic, family, friendships, even financial relationships. When I say financial, I am talking about your relationship with money.

One relationship I want to specifically mention is the one with yourself. Yes, I have already said this I know, but I will keep saying it. Mindset is everything and very precious.

By this I mean looking after you. Not just physically, but mentally too. At 21 I was not aware of the idea of looking after yourself. I was fine, of course.

I do not know about you, but I had that mentality that I was untouchable.

How wrong was I?

I was fit and a happy-go-lucky person.

I feel that being in business and life in general can zap these feelings out of you. Even if we are not aware of this at the time.

I am not doom and gloom about business but I want to be real with you and I am not going to pretend being in business is a bed of roses.

If you are in business, I am sure you already know this.

It has given me a great life and I am so grateful for everything I went through and felt. I just wish I had someone who could have guided me to not allow my mental health to suffer.

As I have said, the first few years were hard. However, in total I would say the first 15 years of business were extremely hard.

To be fair to myself I did not know what I was doing!! I was not taught in college how to run a business and I did not really plan a business either. Let's say I was completely 'winging' it and not a plan in sight!

I would say Beauty was something I started as a hobby, that turned into a business. It is only now I realise if I had gone into this with a plan or a mentor, business would have been easier and life would have been sooooo much smoother.

Maybe you can relate to what I am saying? Of course anything is difficult when we do not have the right tools or knowledge.

This brings me back to this book and the reasons why I wanted to write it. I want to talk about creating the right tools and making people aware it does not have to be as difficult as it sometimes feels.

Running a Beauty business is not part of the curriculum for Beauty Therapy. We are not taught how to run a business at college.

Yes some areas can be briefly touched upon, but these areas could be covered in far more detail. This would certainly make things a little easier, I am sure.

I believe, many people see the Beauty Industry as something you do if you are not as academic as others. However, people who think and say this have no clue do they?

Often, people leave college and become self-employed straight away. It is an industry that seems to naturally feed into self-employment. Being employed in the industry is maybe another book. But for now, I am talking about being self-employed or being in business.

When running a business being aware of things that can happen is key to being a success. When I talk about success, I mean having a business that fits with your life. I know there can be so many definitions of success. But, for me, success is being able to have a balance.

'Don't get so busy making a living, you forget to make a life'.

This is something many do not think of. I know I did not.

When I started my business, I was told:

'In order to make a success of being self-employed you work every hour; it is just what you do when you are self-employed'.

I believe this is the worst piece of advice and the biggest mistake people who are self-employed or creating a business can make.

If we work every hour available to us think about how many things around us suffer. That includes the relationship with yourself and your family. Think about how much you must sacrifice to dedicate every hour to your business.

Please do not get me wrong dedicating time is, of course, essential. However, it all comes back to balance and planning.

When we plan and have a strategy, we can be more aware of when we need to dedicate time to things, and it also keeps us on track and focused.

I will keep repeating this because I want to make sure you do not fall into the ways that I did before I knew better. I believed what everyone told me. It was coming from a good place. However, these people had never been self-employed!! Think about that for a second.

There are many casualties that can occur when we are running a business/being self-employed. I want to chat about ways to prevent these casualties from happening and make you aware of some of them too.

This book will, no doubt, include some casualties along the way and I hope they just make you think of ways you can prevent them. One of the main things to take a battering can be your own mental health.

Many reasons can cause this and sometimes they creep up on you. Often this kind of mental health decline can be caused by stress.

When we feel stressed and seemingly unaware of how stressed we are it can lead to relationships breaking down in so many ways.

I hope you never feel this way and I hope this book may well help you identify when you may need to take a little extra care of yourself. It goes back to when you are on an aeroplane. Put your own mask on first, before helping others. When YOU are ok, you can provide a better service for others.

If you are reaching burnout your business and clients can suffer and then ultimately you are paying the price. Being in the Beauty Industry you can be exposed to many stress triggers such as:

- Working with people - Both clients and staff. The accountability stops with you. You can have to deal with unpredictable circumstances; altering your daily plans,
- Negativity - The customer is NOT always right, listen to feedback and unfortunately more people will tell you the negatives over the positives. My advice is spin this on its head, take this feedback and become the BEST salon.
- High work intensity – The workload never stops. Keeping on top of things is hard; balance and planning are key.
- Perfectionism - Being the best we can be. We have higher expectations of ourselves than anyone, causing extra stress; perfection is impossible. Go easy on yourself!
- The need to please - We want clients to leave happy. You feel responsible and any comeback is on you to deal with.
- Emotions from clients - We listen to their stories and take on their feelings; we act like a counsellor without the skills. It is hard not to want to fix them.
- The pressure on how you look - You represent your business and the industry itself dictates how we should look. This is a hard image to live up to.

- Lack of Support - You don't have the benefits of big corporations where they have staff benefits; we must take care of that. I never thought of this.
- Overwhelm - This is only natural, although it creeps up. It all starts well, and I truly believe this is a massive trigger because it is not something we expect.

When you are in business, you may think:

'I am my own boss; I can do what I want when I want and there is nobody to answer to.'

Please rethink this!

Your clients are your bosses and there are lots of them. So now you have more bosses than you ever did before.

You may disagree, but if clients are not happy they do not come back, they do not recommend you and then you do not have an income. It is important to think differently about being self-employed or in business.

This is why you must have strong boundaries in place.

If everyone started a business with boundaries in place, things would be much easier.

There are many reasons you may not have boundaries firmly in place:

- Lack of confidence and we do not know any difference
- Scared the client will not come back if we say no
- We do not want to upset anyone (forgetting all about ourselves, of course)
- We are there to serve, so we do not mind putting ourselves out (so wrong here)

There is always a reason. Please think about them though. Are they reasons or are they 'fear talking?'

There is nothing wrong with admitting that by the way. It is important to be honest with yourself.

Did you run a business before starting your Beauty Business? I know I hadn't.

Also, when you start in business, you possibly do not have staff and are running a loan ship. Fantastic, but when you are alone and responsible for everything you can end up taking any client over not having one.

This is just in case another does not come through the door. Right?

But this is when you are not focused on your ideal client. You are not focused on who you want to attract into your Beauty Salon.

It screams desperation. This is not an insult I have done it too. I just want you to really think about it.

My advice

'Do not devalue yourself, or the industry'

Easy to say I know, but if everyone started business how you see it running in your future it would make things so much easier in the long run.

Not every business will be a success but we can work together to make sure yours is. We do this by:

'Reverse engineer your goals'

If you have not heard of this, it means start with what you want to achieve first and then work backwards.

For example...

If you want to work 25 hours per week in your salon and make said amount of profit, you need to reverse engineer how that happen.

How much would you need to earn per hour?
What treatments do you offer to make it possible?
Do you have another stream of income you could add in?

If not what can you begin to put in place to make this happen?

The reason we reverse engineer is because otherwise it is easy to get stuck on that 'rat wheel', as I call it. Just working 'in' your salon day in and day out and not making progress because you are 'too busy'. I get it, I really do. But it is important to break the cycle.

Take that day off and start planning for your future. I am sure you did not start your business to have 'a job'. Because I bet if you really worked out your profit margins and your wages it is possibly one of the worst paid jobs you have ever had.

Not to mention one of the hardest.

Business does not have to be soul destroying. Deep I know. But I have been there and now I work 2 days a week in my salon and that is just because I want to.

Having a business can be very lucrative but it is not easy money.

If you are working 12-hour days and not seeing a profit, something is not right; look at your pricing structure. I hear you saying, 'you do not understand, Louisa, I live in a village and I cannot increase my prices, people will not pay'.

I do not want to say you are wrong, because that is quite rude. But I really feel you are. My salon is in a village too and one of my most popular treatments is my £99 facial.

I know you will come across objections to pricing and people are entitled to their opinion.

Everyone thinks they know best but they are not aware of your costs and your over heads and at the end of the day you need to earn a living too.

So much more goes into pricing than people realise. People rarely take into consideration training costs, reinvesting money into more training as well as into the business itself. This is not even including your level of expertise too. It is far more intricate than just the cost of the treatment and your wages.

This is where my Creating Salon Success group can help too. Pricing can make or break a business. There is no point in working your bum off for minimum wage. This is a big topic and one I am sure you can see I am passionate about. This is because I started with college prices!!

The first massive mistake I made. But this is because I did not know. One thing I will tell you though, trying to increase those prices was very hard. When I had been working at those prices people could not see why I could not do it anymore.
I was working 12 hour days, every day and barely anything to show for it except absolute exhaustion. Please learn from my mistakes.

This will be repeated many times, but it is the best way to reinforce things into your mind. But this chapter is not about pricing it is about casualties. I have mentioned these things because, believe me, they are all linked to damaging your mindset.

Having a strong mindset is key for a successful business and that is hard to maintain. There are so many tools we need to have in place to keep our mindset and not to become disheartened when business is tough.

This is why a mentor is good to have in your corner. But you have to be open to try things. Not everything will work but the advice usually comes from a place of expertise and experience.

Once again, I know this all sounds very doom and gloom. It is not. It is what it is and we must use the tools available to make a successful life and business.

This book is just a small step into being insightful into business. I hope it provides you with some funny stories and some tools to help understand you better; what your passions are and discover your values to help you Create Salon Success.

PORN

So far, this book has been serious, however I did promise a few funny stories and a real 'day in the life of a Beauty Therapist'.

You may be thinking why this chapter is titled 'Porn'. Let me explain…

This was back in 2007. I always diverted the salon phone to my mobile. Nowadays, I would only recommend this to a separate mobile, but back in the day I did not know any different and this is what I did.

Anyway, I was driving through Sheffield. I always remember where I was when I received this particular phone call. The reason being is because I was so shocked, I had to pull over.

Of course, I was on my hands free, but still I needed to stop. You will see why in a minute.

So, I was in an area of Sheffield called Heeley, I was heading back to Aston where my salon was and still is based.

The phone call started with a man asking if I had ever considered renting out my salon for films. I could earn an income.

Now you know how hard we work in Beauty Therapy; I was intrigued by what he had to say.

He started to say:

> 'I am sure you are aware that black on white is extremely popular right now'

Firstly, why would I know this? However, I am sure you can appreciate when I say I had to pull over!!

I have to say I was in shock but still intrigued by the conversation. I could not stop speaking to him. I even started to ask questions. You may be thinking I would have just hung up. And I totally get you. I have no explanation, except shock and intrigue.

You may be thinking what questions did I ask?

Well, I will tell you.

I asked how much it would be? It was £500 for 2 hours! Now how long would it take for us to earn that money? Especially back in 2007.

Of course, there was no way I would do it but I still kept asking more things and in fairness the man answered everything. He was lovely and not in a sleazy way as you may think.

I started to think 'this is a business', just different to mine. He just needed to find a location to host his movie. I kind of wanted to help him out.

It is my personality to want to help people. But porn? Oh no I couldn't!! Could I?

I kept asking my questions:

'I feel conscious having people in my salon, would I just leave you in there?'

You can stay and watch if you like, we have nothing to hide. We are happy for whatever you want to do.

Oh, my goodness, I could feel myself going red as I was still sat in the car.

'Who would clean up?'

Do not worry we have industrial cleaners, and we will leave it how we found it. You have nothing to worry about.

I had to quickly wrap this call up, as I was still in disbelief. I told my husband and he just found it hilarious. I told my Mum and Dad, and they were saying 'you are NOT even thinking about this!'. I found it all funny.

The guy on the phone was so nice that is the only reason I even tolerated the conversation, but obviously reality kicked in and there was no way I would go ahead with it. I had a reputation to uphold, of course.

My clients, now, find my stories hilarious. I am not sure it would be the case if I actually let it happen.

This has to be the craziest and weirdest conversation I have ever had. Now, think what you like. I just saw this as a business transaction. However, when my brain got back to reality, of course, 'I rang him and said I would love to help, but I can't, sorry'.

He said, 'no problem, we have now got the original salon anyway, but thank you'. So, after all my wanting to help and feeling bad that I would not be able to they found somewhere else. I often wonder which salon in Sheffield they got to do it. I guess I will never know.

But, again, this is like a lesson it itself. When something does not work for you, you can say no. You do not have to give reason. It is your absolute right! No guilt…

I mean, when he found somewhere else, he did not feel guilty did he?

Does this sound familiar to parts in your life or business?

THE START OF MY TRAVELS

Whilst I was in Jersey, in the Channel Islands I worked in the travel industry. Funny how things turn out isn't it? If only that careers teacher could see my success now?

It started as a summer job in a hotel. After one year of being in Jersey I gained a job I had dreamed of. I had always seen holiday reps around and about and this job just seemed so exciting.

They got to show people this amazing island and made sure the guests had a fabulous time whilst on their holiday. Not only that, but they also had a car and a mobile!!

This was 1998 and do not forget, mobiles were not big back then. That is a lie, they were huge!! But only in size, not in the amount of people having them!

I passed my driving test whilst in Jersey January 1998. I got an opportunity to have an interview for a holiday rep job at Thomas Cook. I was too young, really, as they only took people over 18. However, the person who interviewed me was from Sheffield. Guess what? Her Mum lived on the same road as my Aunty. We built a common ground, and I got the job! I cannot tell you how exciting this was.

Looking back, from early on in my career journey I always seemed to manage to overcome and achieve in situations that seemed impossible. Little did I realise, all these things set me in good stead for starting my own business later.

Holiday rep jobs were seasonal, so I had to find work in the winter months. Many people in Jersey often went over to Thailand or exotic places. This to me, seemed so exciting. I wanted to do it too. But, in true Louisa style I ended up going away for 15 months instead.

It was September 1999; I was 19 and travelled to Indonesia and Australia. This was incredible. Bali is still one of my favourite places and I cannot wait for an opportunity to go back.

When I got to Australia in December 1999, I travelled, enjoyed the millennium and spent the next year working and travelling. You guessed it I worked for Thomas Cook. Now, I would love to tell you all about my travels, but maybe that is another book!

I returned to the UK. I tried to stay but ended up going back to work in Jersey as a holiday rep for a further six months. Jersey is amazing and the people I know there are incredible, however, the house buying situation is restrictive and rightly so.

I decided I needed to grow up a bit and go back to the UK to stay. This time I was determined I would stay and put down some roots. I guess I felt like I should live that 'normal life'.

Not really my style, but I felt I wanted to. Now after having all this time out of education, I still did not know what I wanted to do. Law was out of the question now in my mind anyway.

I decided I needed to do something that would help me get some friends. Crazy I know, but I had come back to the UK and all my friends had settled down. We were still friends; I just felt a million miles away from everyone.

I had been living a completely different lifestyle. Sometimes I wonder why I ever came back as I really found it hard. Nobody seemed to understand me, and I felt like everyone thought I was strange and vice versa.

I cannot explain why, and it is not meant as a negative. Sometimes, looking back I think I was trying to fit a square peg into a round hole. But, as I have said, I seem to always be able to overcome the impossible. Aged 21 I unintentionally embarked on a new career and went to college to learn Beauty Therapy.

I decided this would be the best course to help me meet people. It worked too. I made a good friend there called Sarah. I lost touch with her, which is a shame. But we were good friends and she will never know how much she helped me settle back in the UK, along with overcoming other things too.

I have always been quite a private person, so I was not always the best at sharing my feelings. This book is skimming the surface really, as it is not about me. It is about my journey into the industry. I just wanted to share some past experiences that I really think have shaped me as a person.

These experiences have helped me create a successful business, stay sane and tell the tale. However, I am not foolish enough to think I did this all alone. I am very much aware of how many people have helped me get to where I am. This is both indirectly and directly. Many may not even realise. However, I will always be grateful.

I hope you can relate to some of my experiences and maybe some of them will inspire you to keep going.

Or help you believe you can achieve your dreams too, even if you do not know what they are.

I can tell you, I never started Beauty Therapy as a career move. I had a job as a PA at Rotherham District General Hospital. I was trying my hardest to fit back in with UK living. This may sound like a weird thing to say. Living abroad is very different. I found settling back in the UK very difficult.

I did struggle to conform to society. I was trying to be 'normal'. I mean living that traditional life. You know the one I said I never wanted! Now I realise I can fit with society as much or as little as I want, but I didn't back then. Again, it is about balance.

Anyway, as usual I digress. The story continues and one day I got a text from a school friend I was still in touch with; however she had settled down and I was not there yet. This was a time I felt very different to many people. I am still, but now I am ok with it. Back then I felt something was wrong with me. I remember thinking it was a strange text to get as it went something like:

> 'If you want to take your nails business further, I'll ring you after work'

A little strange from a friend, do you agree? Anyway, I was intrigued, so I said yes, I'll speak to you later. Another thing I will be forever grateful for.

I am still in touch with this girl today, however, this is a friendship that dwindled and I distanced myself from her because of how I was feeling.

Such a shame and I do not think she ever knew what was going off for me. However, it is all part of growing as a person. We are still in touch and that is nice, our lives are just in different stages.

This leads to my first experience of the 'law of attraction'. Think about yours and if you do not know about law of attraction, you will find out more soon. For now, simply put:

> 'The Law of Attraction is the ability to attract into our lives whatever we are focusing on.'

Ok, I have spoken enough about me, for now, and the doom and gloom of business. I want to start to look at you and what you want out of your business and your life.

ALL ABOUT YOU…

Who am I? This is a question I want you to ask yourself. By this I mean find what are you about?

What do you stand for and what are you values and beliefs? You may be wondering why I am asking you this.

When you understand what makes you tick, you live a more fulfilled life and can create THE most successful business too. Success does not happen by accident. It is very intentional. It takes planning and structure.

When we have a reason for existing it can change our entire outlook on life. It changes why we do things. It changes what we are willing to accept. It can help us be strong with our boundaries.

You are probably thinking, where do I start?

A good place to start is reflection. This is about looking at you. Look inside you!!

It is important to analyse yourself and learn what makes you tick.

We need to look at every one of your qualities, imperfections, impressions you give others, the entire part.

Understanding and accepting everything about you is crucial. This includes what could be seen as flaws too. This does not mean to say they are flaws though.

Ask yourself:

- What are your qualities?
- Your blemishes?
- Do you like who you see in the mirror?
- Do you believe that your identity matches who you see?
- How does that make you to feel?
- Which aspects of your life you are miserable about?
- Where could you make improvements?

Look inwardly as well as externally. Try not to just mask over the issues. I know I have done this. This is what I describe it as burying my head in the sand.

When you understand you, your why and your purpose, it helps keep your boundaries in place and learn to say no!

When everything is in alignment, we can just flow. We will deep dive into this during this book. I believe the best way to run a business is to have your mindset in THE best place it can be.

It also creates that work life balance many of us crave and when we are in business this can be lacking.

VALUES

Understanding who you are and what you are about can come back to your values. Many people know their core values, but have you ever looked deeply into this?

You can find your values if you ask yourself questions. Values are the principles and beliefs by which we live our lives and make our decisions.

If you want to effectively lead yourself and lead others, then you need to be aware of what those values are.

Our values are also linked to how we feel. Think for a moment: are you feeling unhappy, distressed, or dissatisfied about something?

Ask yourself these questions below and it can help identify your core values.

If you found out you only had 30 seconds to live and you can re-live a handful of special moments from your past, what would they be and what makes them so meaningful to you?

....
....
....
....

Looking back at the moments where you were most proud of the work you or your team did, why exactly do you feel that way? On the flip side, what makes you most frustrated or angry?

....
....
....
....

Think of an important decision you had to make that ultimately didn't sit well in your mind. What's the source of that conflict and what could you have changed?

....
....
....
....

When you were young, what did you love doing and why? Do you still do these things and if not, why? What are your passions now and why are you drawn to them?

....
....
....
....

Looking back at when you've overcome really difficult situations in your life, what got you through those times?

....
....
....

What themes arise when you think about times when you've grown the most emotionally?

....
....
....

When you think about other organisations/people you admire and dislike. Think about why and what makes you feel that way?

....
....
....

Thinking back to previous companies you've worked for, what did you love about how they operated?

....
....
....

Think of five people you respect immensely and five you do not trust. How would you describe each person using just one word?

....
....
....

When you're excited about something outside of work that gives you energy and enthusiasm, what makes you feel so passionate?

....
....
....

How would you to describe your work? How decisions are made, priorities and the mindset of your work, what would you say?

....
....
....

Imagine your company grows quickly and exceeds your financial goals. What else do you want to say you accomplished?

....
....
....

Below is a list of words. Circle the 3 that resonate with you the most:

Achievement	Honesty	Professionalism
Ambition	Humour	Punctuality
Caring	Individuality	Quality
Charity	Innovation	Recognition
Collaboration	Intelligence	Relationships
Creativity	Intuition	Reliability
Curiosity	Joy	Resilience
Dependability	Kindness	Risk-taking
Empathy	Knowledge	Safety
Encouragement	Leadership	Security
Enthusiasm	Learning	Self-control
Ethics	Love	Service
Excellence	Loyalty	Spirituality
Fairness	Making a difference	Stability
Family	Motivation	Success
Friendships	Optimism	Thankfulness
Flexibility	Open-mindedness	Traditionalism
Freedom	Passion	Understanding
Fun	Perfection	Wealth
Generosity	Performance	Well-being
Growth	Personal development	Wisdom
Happiness	Popularity	
Health	Power	

You may be wondering why I am suggesting you understand your true values.

Well, there are many benefits to identifying them.

These include:

- **Gives you purpose:** Your values help you understand what is important to you. When something does not align with your values, you may not see the point in doing it.
- **Changes your behaviours:** It keeps your boundaries in check too. If you are usually a yes person, knowing your values may encourage you to say no to something.
- **Making better decisions:** If something does not align with your values, it will help you decide faster and better.
- **Which job works for you:** If your values are in place, it can lead you to the right career path. For example, Beauty may not fit with your values.
- **Increasing your confidence:** When you know what you want and what's important to you, it is so empowering, and you cannot be swayed.

These all sound great, don't they? I hope you can understand how knowing your values can help you in business too.

Boundaries are something we will talk about more because values keep your boundaries firmly in place.

Someone once asked me what I value more?

Time or Money

Sounds simple to answer, doesn't it? I found this so hard.

The reason being, if I said money, it felt greedy. If you are a member of my Creating Salon Success group, you will have done lots of work on this mindset about money.

This is such a predisposed view on money and sometimes what society has created.

Hmmmm...

However if I said time, it is pointless without money. This question has stayed with me, and it is something I recommend asking yourself and really thinking about. Your values really come into play here. This person, said to me.

'Sometimes you have to think would it be worth sacrificing some money to have more time doing what you want to do'.

Believe it or not, this statement was a pivotal point in my business. It made me think I will take that day off to focus on my passion of skincare and I will build on that. By this point I had systems in place.

My staff are amazing, and they do not NEED me. We all work well together and yes, by having an extra day off money would be sacrificed.

However, this money could be made up if I put the same effort into my LA Skincare brand.

Guess what??? It worked!!!

I was now working less at the salon. This is something I had wanted to do for a long time, but I was scared. I did not want to upset clients or staff. I did not want to feel judged. I did not want people to think I could not be bothered any more. The list continues. Can you see the pattern that forms in my brain?

Already I am deciding what people think. I am almost giving them permission to think it too.

This is where your mindset comes into play again. We need to stay strong. Not working in my salon as much gave me the opportunity to work on my Training Academy as well as my Skincare. Two of my passions which I had held off pursuing because I was worried about other people.

Ten years I had been qualified in teaching before I committed to it. Imagine how much further on I would be with my Training Academy if I had pursued it back then. However, I am not sorry about this. I had a big learning curve to go on. I believe in timing and things aligning.

By speaking to the right people and having some mentoring (so much later than I should have) I managed to make changes. They were big changes too.

Remember I worked 12 hours per day for a long time. I still never seemed to have any money though. I am not a spender, so it was not that I frittered it away.

I just had so much wrong. Sad, but true. But you know what, I am here to tell the tale, support other Beauty Salon Owners and I cannot tell you how happy that makes me.

I now work 2 days a week in my salon. This is through choice and I spend my time in my members group, which I love and growing my Skincare range more, as well as expanding my Training Academy.

I am so grateful that I am able to do this.

FRILLY PANTS MAN

I have always had male clients, however, nowadays I tend to keep it to client's partners. Mainly people that are already known to the salon.

A few years ago a gentleman made an appointment for a back massage. Even from the phone call something felt wrong and I should have trusted my instincts. However, I never like to judge people. So I booked the appointment.

I know you are wondering why I felt something was wrong. The reason why, was because he was very umming and ahhhing on the phone, with a few stutters. Now this alone is not a problem. I thought he may have just been nervous. But something just did not feel right. He booked in as Mr Smith.

Saying:

    'Yes, my name is Smith, that is right Mr Smith'

With a few coughs in between.

It sounds quite innocent now, but do you ever feel that something is not right?

I had staff, but on the day of his appointment I was working alone. I worked next door to a hairdresser and I even went there and asked them to send their junior round for the time the massage was due to end. I cannot explain it, I just felt uncomfortable.

Anyway, the gentleman arrived for his appointment. He filled out his record card and of course his name was not Mr Smith!! This should have been my first alarm bell. I did ask him about it and in that familiar nervous voice, he said he felt a little nervous on the phone. I accepted him at his word and thought fair enough.

I took him through for his massage and during the treatment he asked if he could take his trousers off. I said, it is not necessary for a back massage. Plus he was already on the bed.

I carried on the treatment and after another couple of minutes he said it again. I had to get my professional head on and said, 'look we have a salon policy and there is not just me that works here, so we all have to be doing the treatments the same.'

He seemed to accept this, however, then continued to mention how he was wearing frilly women's pants and he enjoyed the way they felt rubbing against him whilst having a massage.

This was another occasion where I think he was just trying to get a reaction.

I just carried on and stayed professional. I knew there was something fishy about him. To be honest I was kind of relieved that is all it was.

He just seemed so cagey and that is what made me uncomfortable. I guess what made it even worse was when he decided to show me his pants and continued to explain how they felt against his body and the sensations he enjoyed whilst being massaged.

I just found it amusing, obviously I did not laugh. This would be rude! But it was a very strange situation.

At this point, I just thought, you know what if he has felt that comfortable telling me it did not bother me. We all have our quirky ways, right?

Anyway, I even asked if he wanted to rebook. Crazy I know!

He said, 'Oh I thought after what I told you I should go somewhere else'. I said, 'well you obviously felt comfortable telling me. So that must have been quite a big thing. So, if it saves you doing it again I am happy for you to book.'

Yes, he booked in again, but he never showed up for the next appointment. I just thought what a bizarre situation.

I was very grateful for having such a good relationship with the hairdressers next door and for her sending her junior round. I believe building relationships is key in business.

Months later I was speaking to someone, and she asked me if I had any funny stories to tell her about my salon. Now, I do not know about you, but I am not one to gossip about my clients as they tell us things in confidence. Plus, I tell clients things too and our relationship becomes one of friendship as well.

Anyway, I decided this was a story I could share. I think it always sounds funnier when it is told in person and out loud. You will have to just imagine that bit. I am into amateur dramatics too. So, you can imagine the theatrics when I tell a story. I have a fabulous group of friends who totally accept all of my theatrics and often call me 'Jazz Hands!'

More time went by and my friend said to me 'Louisa, you know that story you told me about frilly pants man?

Well, my friend has a salon and she told me the exact same story last night'. It turns out she had seen him recently. It must now be a year since I had seen him.

We worked out he seemed to just go around different salons in the nearby area and do the same thing.

My friend was a police officer at the time, and she decided to log it as intel as it was very bizarre behaviour.

Now, fast forwarding a few years. I had sold that building I was in and began to sublet again 1 mile up the road.

I had been there a couple of weeks and I was settling in. This place was above a hairdresser and one of the ladies came over and asked me if I could speak to a gentleman about massage.

Well, I could not believe my eyes it was him!!!

Of course, I recognised him straight away. I have no idea how or why. Obviously, he stuck in my brain.

He asked me the price of a massage. I just told him £50 for half an hour. It was not, but I did not want him in again. No other reason than it was not genuine, and I was not in the mood to give him a reaction.

I decided to tell him I recognised him, and his name just popped into my head. I said 'oh you are Mr .... ' I still feel I should keep his name private, just because I respect the rules. Well, this was one of those occasions I wish I had a camera as his reaction was absolutely priceless.

He seemed to recognise me too, once he knew I knew him. He even remembered where my old salon was. This amused me even more. I was much older now. I actually think 6 years must have gone by.

So, he clearly did this a lot.

Each to their own, but I think this is quite sad and quite rude and disrespectful to our industry.

It is amusing and the story is funny.

However, I started to realise the potential seriousness of this the second time around. I can handle myself, but what if this happened to someone quite vulnerable? Or to my staff when they were working alone?

When I saw him the second time, I really wanted to book him in with my Mum as she would have set him straight. However, this was all good in hindsight.

Ok, so now I am typing this story, it may not be so funny. But please take it in the light-hearted way it is meant.

Also, a lesson in dealing with situations.

Not to mention a reminder on we can say NO!

We do not have to book people in if we feel uncomfortable. We do not have to justify why. I mean, look, I felt uncomfortable on the telephone.

My gut instincts were right. I should not have booked him in. If this had had been a staff member, I would have felt awful.

My lesson here is, listen to your instincts and do not feel bad if you decide you are not booking someone in.

We often feel like we should book everyone in our salon. But think about your ideal customer. Not everyone is and we should feel comfortable in our job.

If someone is making us feel uncomfortable, then say no.

Remember to keep those boundaries firmly in place. Do not feel guilty. After this story, if you choose not to accept male customers, I really do not blame you!

I still accept male customers, but only people I know or that are known to the salon.

I have an obligation to my staff, and we have an obligation to ourselves.

Ok I think I have stressed my point here.

I am very conscious of putting my staff in vulnerable situations too and this is something we need to think about when employing staff as we do have a responsibility towards them too.

ALIGNMENT

Values are your core beliefs and understanding your core beliefs and why we do what we do helps everything fall into place.

I believe that when things are working or you are on the right path, everything aligns. Basically, I mean things are easy and everything seems to fall into place.

When we find we must fight for something or things do not seem easy, it can make you reassess if this is right.

Many times, I have tried hard to achieve something and many times I have managed it. However then I would often look back and think maybe I should have looked at why it seemed so difficult to achieve.

Was it my best move? Or was the universe trying to put me on a different path and I refused?

It is always good to ask yourself questions. I always say my goal is the same but sometimes I may need to adapt my journey.

It is not a bad thing. In business I believe it is important to be adaptive when situations arise or our path needs to change course a little.

You may be wondering, what does it matter? And how can we tell if we are aligned?

These are just my opinions, everyone is different and that is absolutely fine.

My thoughts are when we are aligned with the universe, it is the inner knowing that we are living life according to the divine plan and not being swayed by society's beliefs for us.

We are living our life in accordance with our true values and our true selves. This means not getting muddled up by all the masks that we need to wear or all of the influences around.

The universe knows when we are living in alignment with our highest self and when we are not. It rewards us or reminds us with signs and signals.

These can be anything from significant lyrics in a song on the radio or that song being repeated over and over. You know when something feels like it is everywhere. Or every time you get in the car you hear a song. These are what I feel are all signs.

This is the universes way of sending messages. They can come at us from all the different avenues. Start looking out for these signs.

When we are not in alignment and we are at the point of being swayed by a media message or we have misaligned ourselves by accepting a job that is not our true calling or marrying someone who is obviously not right for us.

The universe sends us warning bells or signals.

Sometimes we can hear the warning signals and other times we do not and yet we still go on our path as we think we know better.

I am often my own worst enemy and really can make my own life so much more difficult than it needs to be.

Can you relate?

There are times we do not see or hear these warning signs at all because we are so unconscious, busy, stressed or out of sorts. I know I have been guilty of this. Have you?

I have noticed that when I am in alignment I am as close to being in the most blissful state I have ever been in. This is a rarity in my world as I am always 100 mph.

This is why it is really important to me that I take time out and do yoga or walk in nature and reconnect.

When I am in alignment, everything feels effortless. This means those times I am not in alignment; everything is just the opposite.

Everything feels hard, very little seems to work out right and everything takes ten times longer and ten times the effort.
I can feel tired, grumpy, unhappy and generally out of sorts with the world.

I know there's something wrong. This is when it is so important to take a step back to understand what is going on.

I am a big fan of angel cards and I feel this is a great way to keep me on track. Certain cards often come out when I am out of sorts.

All those ones telling me to take time out in nature or to do more yoga. It helps me assess where did I misalign myself?

What happened and why?

I believe we can tell we are aligned when all these seemingly random coincidences keep on happening without any real influence from us.

Being out of alignment does not mean everything is wrong it is just sometimes a way to make you step back and reassess things.

Can you think back to a time this has happened? Either in business or personal life?

This all comes back to your goals and your why. This we will talk about very soon. However, for now, make a few notes here.

Really try and think back to times when everything has been going right and then think when things haven't.

Please make some notes here:

YOUR WHY!

I just mentioned your why. What do I mean? I know many people will say I do it for my children and my family.

However, I feel like your why is deeper than that. I understand that is why we do what we do but let's attempt to look at this a little differently.

The WHY is the purpose, the cause or the belief that drives every one of us to do what we do every day.

The whole concept of WHY is grounded in the deep beliefs in our brain. It is like it is in our internal make up. Often, we look at: How, What, Why?

The 'how' in business and personal life include strengths or values you feel differentiate you from the competition. It connects with the limbic brain; the part that controls behaviour and emotion.

'What' you do is often easier to articulate as it is you talking about your treatments or services you offer. The 'What' engages with the neocortex; the rational part of our brain.

Successful people and businesses express 'why' they do what they do rather than focusing on what they do. This is something that is really worth thinking about.

This is what can make people want to come to your salon because they connect with you and what your business is about.

Your 'Why' is a way to communicate with the listener's limbic brain; the part that processes feelings such as trust, loyalty, and decision making.

When you are working in alignment with your why it gives you a drive to move forward in both your business and your personal life.

Always start with why. It is how you explain your purpose and the reason you exist and behave as you do and to pursue the things that give you fulfilment.

Your why will serve as your point of reference for all your actions and decisions and helps you to measure your progress and know when you have met your goals.

When you are not doing what you love or feel of importance, it can be draining. Can you relate? Days can drag when we are not motivated, and it leads to a lack of fulfilment.

Finding your 'why' is important for both your wellbeing, mentally and physically.

Look within, discover the things that you are passionate about, and pursue them. Regardless of other people's doubts or the setbacks you will meet.

The secret to a long and happy life is to live by 'your why' every day. For those who are part of my Creating Salon Success membership site, you will have heard me talk about the Japanese concept of Ikigai.
This is such a wonderful tool to doing this. It can take some time to discover your reason for being. But be patient.

The Japanese have the term Ikigai, which can be translated to mean a reason for being. This is anything that gives a deep sense of purpose to a person's life and makes it worthwhile. It is what you get up for every morning.

Ikigai helps you find your personal why, your reason for being, which is important because that will bring your passion for your business, as we can get lost in society and media.

You may be wondering what the heck am I talking about?

According to Ikigai there are four questions you need to answer. Answer the following questions to help you reach your why.

Come back to this time and time again. It is a useful tool but can take some time, like everything it is not a one-time wonder. It takes work and continuous practice and focus.

This can keep you motivated.

1) **What do you love? This is to figure out what you find fun, interesting and motivating**

What would you do if you didn't have to worry about money?
How would you spend your time on a long holiday or weekend?
What's excites you and gets your juices flowing when you do it?
What could you enthusiastically talk about for hours on end?

....
....
....
....

2) **What the world needs? What you can give to the world, culture, or your family.**

Who and what inspires you?
What issues in world touch you emotionally?
Do people part with their resources to buy what you're selling?
Will your work still be relevant a decade from now?

....
....
....
....

3) What you are good at your natural gifts, your talents and skills.

What parts of your current job are you effortlessly good at?
What are you the best in your workplace/community at?
What extra education and experience could you do with?
What do people ask for your help with?

....
....
....
....

4) What you can be paid for whether you enjoy them or not.

Have you been paid for what you do?
If not, are other people being paid for this work?
Are you already making a good living at what you do?
Can you eventually make a good living doing this work?

....
....
....
....

Someone once said to me. A good way to look at your 'why' is to think about what you would like your legacy to be.

When you die, what do you want to be remembered for?

Your why is extremely important and when you work in alignment with your why and your values, it helps you in many ways.

It helps you to:

- Learn to say no
- Create boundaries
- Keep a strong and healthy mindset

MY FIRST EXPERIENCE OF LAW OF ATTRACTION

Remember I mentioned the text from my friend?

Now, she had messaged me about taking my nails business further.

Bear in mind nails was never my passion and it still isn't.

However, I once saw a nails shop (in my village) and I said to my Mum, 'gosh I wish I could just sit and do nails all day instead of admin.'

I had never heard of the Law of Attraction. But it was working! Law of Attraction does not decipher whether it is your path it just listens to what you say. I never said, 'I would like to do that, just not nails.' I was not specific I just wanted to do that... and what that was, was nails.

I had brought it on myself. Funny now. Anyway, as quick as this nails shop opened, it closed too.

But I still thought this would be great. It just seemed different I guess and maybe it would give me some sort of normal working life. How wrong. But we will address this later.

Back in 2001, there was not a salon on every corner, like today. I was the first Sole Beauty Salon to open in my village.

Every other salon was within a hairdressers. It was as if Beauty Salons were not a stand-alone business back then.

My friend, true to her word, rang me and I will always be grateful for that phone call.

Someone she knew was opening a tanning studio and they wanted someone to do nails! Well, it was like it was magic. I said it and the next thing it was a possibility.

I did not know about Law of Attraction back then, but I know, now. And believe me, it works!! I have so many examples like this.

I decided I had nothing to lose. I was still at college so would not want to commit full time, but I could do evenings and weekends. I began by performing nail and feet treatments at a tanning studio in my village.

It worked well from the start.

Possibly because I was charging college prices!! Oh, how wrong this was, but I did not know any different.

There was no surprise I would be busy charging those prices. The effort to increase these prices were immense. My advice is start as you mean to go on. Do not do what I did.

Another lesson I learnt, however I gained loads of experience!! I have to take the positive out of a situation.

BEAUTY BY LOUISA WAS BORN

I remember so many people, at the time, saying 'aren't you brave?'. I did not really understand this statement. I do now.

But back then I was somewhat carefree.

I still am, I guess, and I always think 'what is the worst that could happen?'

Aged 21 and I guess this could be what you could class as my first break. The tanning studio I was doing nails in, also had a room to rent.

I did not want to be doing nails, so, I took the room on as well and began offering facials and massage.

This was great and I realised very quickly, this was the part of the business I loved.

I named the business 'Beauty by Louisa' and within a few months I left my PA job to focus on the business full-time.

What had I got to lose, really? If only I knew then, what I know now. I had so much to lose.

Not necessarily financially, which is what they meant when they said, 'aren't you brave?'. I did not have the responsibilities others may have had. It was more about me as an individual. I lost touch with life in general and I lost touch with me. What I wanted out of life and my mental health suffered too. If only I had a mentor or a guide to help me!

However, the things I did not take into consideration were things I had never really thought about before. Some little tips I would say to you when starting out or even before you start are:

>'Don't lose your self-worth'

>'Don't work so much you resent your business'

>'Remember to have a life!'

>'Be aware of burn out!'

>'Get a coach, but someone who knows what they are doing and has done it!'

>'People will walk all over you if you let them'

>'Have faith in yourself'

>'Clients will come and go; it is not personal'

>'You will never please everyone all of the time – but you should please you'

>'Clients are not always right'

The business took off straight away. I was the first sole Beauty salon in the area. The tanning studio I was renting in quite quickly started to dwindle.

Not because it was not a good business. This was at a time, when the tanning industry had gone from being at its peak, to starting to fade out. Excuse the pun.

The people I was renting off had asked me if I wanted to buy their business as they were going to moving away. To be honest, I did not want to take on another business and I also did not want to pay out for a business. Especially one I had no interest in.

However, I knew this was potentially going to cause me a problem. I had a very busy salon and my client base had grown so much. I did not know what I was going to do. This was quite daunting and scary.

I tried to take over the lease, but that would not work. The current tenants, who I was subletting from wanted to sell their business, which was understandable. It was not for me though.

I do not want to go into detail too much here. But this was a very difficult time for me. This was the start of when I realised how nasty being in business could be and what broad shoulders you needed.

Someone once referred to me as naive. I remember thinking 'I have travelled the world; I am not naive!'. Well, I think they may have been correct, maybe I was, especially where business was concerned!!

During this period, I realised you must look after yourself. People have not always got your back. Even when you do not expect it, true colours are shown.

That saying springs to mind:

> 'People often forget what you do for them, but always see what you don't'

Even as I type this, I am hesitant because many negative and anxious feelings start to come up. Things I thought I had dealt with. I am skirting around the edges here. It is a long story and I do not feel it is right for this book. However, it did give me a strong start into the business world.

This was a time I realised what people could be like and even when you try to do 'the right thing' it does not always work.

I was 23 here and felt like I was a strong character and knew it all. I realised here I knew nothing about how people could be with you. Let's call it a big learning curve.

Just remember though it is your life, and you must live it for you. If you can hold your head high and know you did not do anything with malicious intent, I believe you are ok.

You cannot please everyone, right?

ENTREPRENEURIAL SPIRIT

You could say my entrepreneurial spirit came to the forefront two years after starting my Beauty business, when nearby premises came up for sale.

Once the tanning shop had decided they were leaving, I felt very stuck.

I would have to find somewhere else. A building on the same road came up for rent. Now, this building was extremely old and did not seem to have been looked after. It smelt too. I always remember that. I thought there was no harm in enquiring.

So, I did. Although I decided to ask if they would sell it. I am not sure where this crazy idea came from. But I knew this building would need so much work, I thought maybe buying it would be a better option.

I did it!! I bought it!! They agreed to my offer and that was that. OMG! What had I done?

Aged just 24, I bought the property on a mortgage. I knew I would find a way to make it work. I'd have got a part-time job cleaning toilets to make ends meet, if necessary.

It worked well I gained staff I lost staff. No hard feelings from me, however I had no clue what I was doing. All I knew was I could do treatments and that was it. I had no clue how to run a business, nor how to deal with staff. I tried and it sort of worked. But I was winging it.

It seemed to be going all right though as clients were still coming back. You know what though, I still was not happy with this kind of normal life. But I carried on, regardless.

Taking on this property was hard. I was so lucky to have the support from my Mum and Dad. I am not sure how I would have done it without them. Not necessarily financial but giving their time to help in so many ways.

This property needed so much doing and again I really did not have a clue. I did what I thought, but I do think I buried my head a lot in the salon. My Mum is and always has been my rock to keep me grounded and focused and pull my head out too!

I was good at treatments and clients came and were happy. So, it all seemed to be working well. For me, though, I was spinning so many plates. I was just doing what I could.

Moving into these premises is a whole story, but a long one.

It was a difficult time to be honest and not the smoothest journey. The business was fine, it was more the move from rented to owning a property. I upset the people I sublet from; this was never my intention.

It was stressful to think what I would do if I did not have a place to run my business from. It turned out they never moved, so it looked like I had now set up in competition with them. Of course, I had not as I had been doing Beauty and they were tanning.

However, once I had left, they began to do Beauty through employing someone. This was no problem to me; I had my client base. But it was a very difficult time. I never like upsetting people, even now.

Anyway, that story is far too deep and long for this book. All I am saying is you must watch your back in business. Do what is right for you.

I do not believe anyone has any intention of upsetting others. Stay focused on you and do not focus too much attention on what others are doing.

I decided to just concentrate on my business and not really give much thought to them. I knew I had not set up in competition. I just wanted a place to do treatments on my clients in and I had this now.

Plus owning somewhere made me think I did not have to ask permission to make changes or expand my business. I could just do what I wanted and what was best for me.

During the time of owning this property I employed staff too. I look back now and think what was I doing? However, one of these staff members stayed with me for over 10 years, so something must have been ok.

Of course, there is a story here, but I will go into more details later.

After 7 years of owning these premises I decided to sell them. It just felt right. I had it up for sale and someone came and made an offer. I decided to accept it. I wanted to go back to Australia, and I had been making plans and exploring opportunities to move there.

This building started to feel like a noose around my neck and I was thinking I had had enough of Beauty and the UK and I wanted to leave. I thought getting rid of this building would be the way for me to do this.

Of course, things did not turn out this way, but we live and learn. It is still on my list and one day it will happen.

Maybe I should just back track here and tell you I was now married. I bumped into one of the lads I worked with at that timber supplies. We became friends again and it went from there. The next thing we are married. Obviously, there is more to that story. But I will save that. The business was doing well, but I was exhausted with it all. Still winging it. Not that I would ever describe myself as a structured person, but I needed structure.

Myself and my husband both wanted to move to Australia, so that was the grand plan. But I had to keep working until this opportunity happened. Getting rid of the building was the priority.

For me to keep running my business I thought I could just go back to subletting. Of course, law of attraction worked again and a place, just up the road came up. This worked great. It also gave me the head space from having staff and running the business and maintaining a building. My passion for Beauty had reignited and I could focus on the business and what I wanted to do.

The next thing I know I am throwing all of my time and energy into developing my skincare brand. I know, you are thinking 'what, where did that come from?'

This had always been a dream of mine, something I had never thought possible. But of course, Louisa can always overcome the impossible and so can you.

This worked so well, better than I could have imagined. So much so that the dream of Australia had just moved a little. This was proving hard, and I needed to create opportunities. The skin care was the next step in my entrepreneurial journey.

I am not going to go into how I created my skincare brand. It was several years and a long story. Again, maybe for another book! However, after numerous years LA Skincare was born.

I had always been told if you are proud of something you put your name to it. Now I already had Beauty by Louisa, and this came with a few problems when I got staff as everyone wanted their Beauty treatments done by Louisa. Which makes sense.

Anyway, I decided this had limited the expansion of my salon and I did not want to do the same to the skincare. I know it is not the same but that was my thinking at the time. I decided to call it LA, standing for Louisa Ashforth. Basically me! This is how the LA brand was born.

Subletting above the hairdressers and I became so busy I needed help. One of the girls who worked for me before started working for me again.

We had always stayed in touch and she was and still is a great therapist. She worked like me. It was great, she just slotted back in. This was great as, again, it gave me more opportunities to progress the skin care range.

After numerous years, once again I needed to move. The business had completely outgrown where I was. I had skincare under beds, and we were trying to do treatments. It just was no longer practical. It was exactly what I needed though.

My dream building, just a little further up the road became available. I had contacted the owner of the property, previously. I wanted to make myself known to him and let him know I was interested if the building ever became available.

Eventually, when it became available he got in touch and I had first refusal. Of course I had to take it!

I decided to change the name from Beauty by Louisa, as I said it was limiting. I had LA Skincare too and I wanted the salon to be linked to it. The new salon name became LA Beauty and Hair.

You may be thinking where did the hair come from? Well, there was already a girl doing hair there and the landlord was worried she would be out of a job. I said she could stay, but under the LA umbrella. This is how hair became in the name.

After a massive refurbishment and many changes the salon has become the spa I always dreamed of. It now has a steam room, sauna, relaxation room, 4 treatment rooms and a hairdresser. It also has a training room for LA Training Academy.

The LA brand is growing.

Anyone who knows me will not be surprised when I say there are still have a few extra additions in the pipeline for the salon too.

WOMB-MAN

This is quite as long on. I will try to be quick.

I once had this guy book in for a back massage. Consultations are something I have always done, and this client was no different.

He sat down in reception. This is not where we did consultations, however, there was only me and him in and he was chatting away.

All I could think was I am running out of time; I haven't even done my consultation yet. You know what it is like, sometimes.

The conversation started by him telling me about his biggest mistake in his life was losing the love of his life. She was in Thailand, and he didn't go with her. I was only 23 at this time and I was patiently listening, whilst inside flapping about timing.

The way he was talking I thought it was something that had happened recently as he seemed upset. As the story unfolded, it turned out to be something that had happened 20 years, prior.

It felt so random, but this should have been my first realisation moment that this was a weird situation. I never like to judge, and I like to think I give everyone a chance.

My patience started to wear thin as I could tell we would be here a while. So, I filled out the consultation card and we went to start the treatment.

I know sometimes doing treatments on men can feel awkward and especially if you are alone in the salon. I was alone at this point, but I did have staff working for me and they were out delivering leaflets, I was not worried as I knew they would be back before the treatment was finished.

He seemed nice enough, anyway.

However, as I was about to start the treatment, he told me that if he made any funny noises or his body shot into different positions or shapes that I should not worry. It is involuntary and it is because when he has a massage, he goes back into his mother's womb! Yes, you read that correctly.

I told you some stories are farfetched, and this has to be the corker, to be honest. I took it with a pinch of salt and genuinely thought 'oh ok love!'

How wrong was I?

At this point, I was convinced I was on TV and Jeremy Beadle was going to pop out. This is no joke. I was determined not to look stupid on TV.

I did the whole massage, and I did not even cut the time down by a minute! In my eyes, at the time, I was ever the professional. Now I just think I was blinking stupid. But hey, what is that saying? You live and learn.

I swear this story will not have the same effect reading it as when I am telling it. But we can only do what we can do can't we?

He was laid on his front and I was massaging his back. Within the first 2 minutes his right arm shot up in the air. I looked and thought 'no way!!' However, like I said, I just carried on. Next the left leg. I can remember it like it was yesterday because it was bonkers.

There was absolutely no reaction from me. And the next thing his bum was rising. Can you imagine? Some weird super man position with some sort of arched back and bum up... I know this is hard to visualise, you need my actions. But please try.

A few other positions came and went, but there was no reaction from me, so these seemed to calm down.

Then came the noises. Lots of oohing and ahhing. Again, I carried on as if nothing was happening. Maybe I did a few eye rolls, but I needed to be professional, remember there was a camera and Jeremy Beadle.

I massaged the side of his back; you know that bit that always feels funny when being massaged? Your Teres Major muscle. I think it can always feel a bit tickly, so I get it. However, his reaction was more like a loud 'oooh, oooh, oooh, aaaaaahhhhh, oooh I wondered why you were massaging there and oooh, oooh, ooh now I know'. A very bizarre reaction, but OK. All is good, I was counting down the time, now. Please hurry, I had had enough now.

These noises carried on until the end.

He asked me if I would massage his hands as he was struggling with them. Of course, I did it. Crazy, I know!

So, I did his hands and there was one of his fingers where he said, 'Oh I don't think you massaged that one'. I couldn't be bothered to argue, so I just did it again, where he proceeded to make a lot of very loud ooh's again. It was almost like an orgasm; it was quiet and then got louder and louder and then a release. I hope that makes sense.

As I am typing this, I am in disbelief I continued the treatment. I just accepted him, but it was weird and don't forget Jeremy Beadle!
The treatment was finally over. He went to the toilet and by this point my staff were back. I said all hands-on deck, we need to strip this room.

There was an underlying smell in there and believe me it was not pleasant. Before COVID times, it was a case of stripping the towels and leaving the bottom sheet. However, everything came off. I even threw away a bolster cushion because it stunk. I cannot explain what this was.

Anyway, bear in mind we had stripped the bed, all the towels and sheets were in the washer. The washer had been started. We had mopped the floor and made the bed again and he was still in the toilet.

I was so distracted by the cleaning; I had not noticed how many times the toilet had flushed and the length of time he was in there. I was just thinking I did not want him to catch us cleaning to such extent as I did not want to make him feel bad about himself.

Well, we had finished and I said to my staff 'if that toilet flushes one more time I am knocking on that door'.

He came out of the toilet and was sat in reception talking to one of my staff. He then told me he would not have her do his treatment because she was only 16. She was an apprentice at college.

I told him this and he told me he did not agree with it. I did find this strange. However, when I went up to the toilet, there was no toilet roll!!! I will leave it to your imaginations. But I was fuming. My salon had been treated with such disrespect. I took pride in my business and my job, and I felt like a knocking shop!

No wonder he thought it was inappropriate to have my 16-year-old do a treatment on him. Honestly, I was disgusted.

This was back at a time I was scared to lose clients, scared to say no, scared to get a bad reputation. I did not put myself first at all. And in this case nor my staff. Which was not good. I mean the guy was nice, but he clearly was not there for the massage Beauty Therapists offer.

You guessed it, there was no Jeremy Beadle either. I told you it was a long one, not to mention a weird one too!!!

The lesson:

I learnt my lesson here. Even I felt uncomfortable and that takes a lot because I usually just laugh at things and I can sometimes be a bit naïve. So I would have just carried on which I did, obviously.

This story is a funny and strange one but one that makes you realise how vulnerable we can be and what situations we can find ourselves in.

My advice here is go with your gut instinct. If you feel uncomfortable, you have every right to feel uncomfortable. Imagine if that treatment had been with my other staff member, I would have felt awful.

People can be so inappropriate, and it can feel like our jobs are not taken seriously.

Once again, boundaries need to be paramount in our job. Which will lead us nicely on to our next chapter.

BOUNDARIES

You may be wondering why we need to set boundaries. Remember at the beginning of this book, how I spoke about mindset and how it is THE most important thing when it comes to a successful business? A healthy mindset can be helped by healthy boundaries.

Boundaries are there for you and they show other people how you want to be treated and what you are willing to put up with.

Well, after reading this I want you to know what your boundaries are, and I want you to put these boundaries into practice.

After all, we are not machines!! Machines are built to work 24/7, we mere humans are not.

It is crucial we take time out for ourselves, for exercise, me time, down time, time with loved ones. This creates a sound and healthy mind and this is why we need to set ourselves boundaries and we need to respect those boundaries, as well as respecting other peoples.

I mentioned your why earlier and we looked at Ikigai. You will notice how everything is linked. If you have heard of Chakras you know when one is out of alignment, something is not right. Well, it is a little bit like that when it comes to mindset.

In order to have a healthy mindset we start by being aware of our values. Knowing our values helps us understand our why and by understanding our why we can set boundaries. All of these help us achieve our goals in life and business, as well. We did not get into business to just stand still. The Beauty world is so fast paced, we cannot stand still, or we will be left behind.

When we have firm boundaries in place, we are strong in mind, and we have the ability and confidence to say no. As Beauty Therapists, we are born to serve. However, this does not mean that we have to say yes to everything.

Someone once said to me: 'Just because you can, does not mean you should'. At the time, I thought that is very selfish. If I can help someone I will. However, I now realise what she meant. I am happy to help others, just not at the detriment of myself and my family.

What is important to me, as in my why, comes first. This means if something is going to take me away from fulfilling my why, which means it will move me further away from achieving my goals, I am going to say no.

We cannot please everyone all the time and the first person you should be looking at pleasing is yourself. You must be able to set boundaries otherwise you are allowing others to dictate what you are doing with your time.

You can still be a nice person and have boundaries. I always want to be liked, so this is obviously a big thing for me.

Would you rather let others decide what you are doing, or would you rather say 'no' to things that do not fit with your boundaries? Solid boundaries can make you become more efficient. Look at others who you admire and look at what they are doing to set boundaries.

It is so easy to get sucked in to doing more clients and putting our family to one side. But we must become really clear on why we do what we do and if we respect our boundaries, others will begin to respect them too. How good does that sound? I am not saying this is easy. It takes practice, so practice saying no.

There are many times in the past I have known my husband is cooking my dinner and then a client has turned up late (meaning I will finish late), or I have squashed that extra appointment in (just because he will understand). Now, it doesn't matter that they understand, is it fair? Is it putting your needs first or is it you putting work first?

This is because I didn't have boundaries or a firm why. However, now, I do not do that. My time with my husband is important. Many times in my marriage I have put work first. It is almost a standing joke that if a client wants something done, I will prioritise them. I can joke, but I do not like that, really!

My marriage is one of my whys. Without my husband, Andy, I would not be able to do what I do, because we are a team. That is why it is so important that I set those boundaries and be clear on my why. Believe me, other people put their why first.

They are happy for you to put your why to one side when it suits them, because it works for them. You have to be strong on your whys.

I can be that person who is completely focused, and it is like the outside world does not exist. Sometimes Andy has said to me 'I think you have forgotten about me.' Now, I joke and say stop being so needy. However, imagine that the other way around. I would not want to feel like I am not a priority.

I am not saying these things to make you feel bad there is no need to dwell on times you have prioritised work and clients over family or other commitments. However, this is your reminder to become focused on your why.

If you are still thinking about your why and you are not sure try looking back at why you became self-employed. Make a list of five to ten reasons.

Maybe things like:

> I will have more time for me
>
> I can get a hobby
>
> I will have time for family and friends
>
> I will have financial freedom
>
> Nobody to answer to
>
> I can do what I want and when I want

One of the biggest things many of us do not have enough of is time.

Let's look a bit deeper and think where do you waste time? Once again, make a list of areas you feel you may waste time in. It could be worth doing a time log of your daily activities.

Do you find yourself scrolling through Tik Tok looking at videos?

Your list of time-wasting activities may include:
- Scrolling social media for hours on end
- Putting clients before your family time
- Squeezing that extra client in when you should have said no
- Getting that extra bit of money in and now you are exhausted
- Making endless cups of tea because you have not got a plan for the day

There is always just one more or yes but that is an extra £20 for my business.

But you need to look and think is that sustainable long term? Does that make the business you dreamed of? Did you dream to work so late and not have any energy or time left?

It is so easy to say yes to everything, just in case!

Boundaries help us start to say no and not feel guilty. Let's look at some areas you could set boundaries to create more time and be very specific with what boundaries you want to set around these areas.

Time is always a good one and it is so important! We need to be recharged, especially if you are a salon owner as it can become exhausting. Get a planner, plan your week and structure your days. This can make all the difference to managing your time better.

Have you ever done a time log? This is a great way to assess where you spend your time, or actually waste your time. You can just use a pen and paper or there are apps too.

Set out appointments with yourself. Sounds crazy doesn't it?

I know someone who actually diarises their sexual activity with their partner. By this I mean they schedule sex in their diary.

This may be a little too far for me but it did make me chuckle, so I thought I would share it with you.

We may laugh, but this person is ridiculously organised and has firm boundaries in place and is incredibly successful. May not be so funny now, hey?

Mine are a little more low key then scheduling private time with my husband. I like to set time aside in a morning for my daily exercise. This is important to me and non-negotiable. It is not necessarily because I want to look good. This is more to do with mental health. My head is always spinning with ideas and always on the go.

I need to de-stress and have time out. This is why this exercise is so important to me. Obviously, I want to look good and feel my best. I feel that running helps me. I joke and say I was not built to run, because it is something I find hard. Yet when I have done it I feel amazing!! I have a treadmill which I use, but if I have chance I prefer to run around a lake which is near where I live.

Another example of putting non-negotiables in place is, having breakfast with my hubby. This is not always possible as he starts work super early, so if Andy has a late start (by late I mean not 6.30am) we can have breakfast together.

Another is I make sure I do not start in the salon (if I am working there) until the opening time.
You know what I mean by that, there are many times I have, in the past, gone in way before opening and stayed way later. Not anymore!!

Even though salon work requires late nights, this is actually the part of the job I dislike the most. I am much more of an early bird, and I would love to work 6am-2pm every day. However, unfortunately salon life does not work that way! But you know something that is the perk of being your own boss. Believe it or not I no longer work late nights or if I ever do they are very occasional.

I now limit the late nights and it feels empowering, because I am living how I want and running my business for me. You know clients will adapt and if they don't, they may not be your target customer and that is ok.

Or have you got staff? Can they do the late night? Mine do. Just because it is your salon, it does not mean you have to be there at every waking moment.

Think about what it is for you, your goals, your why, and your life. Have you heard of preservation goals? These are things that you are not prepared to sacrifice. It could be you always put your children to bed. Or having that spa day once a month or taking that walk you love. Set time aside in your diary. Get crystal clear on your boundaries.

For example, I love holidays, this is something that means a lot to me. These should be on your planner and booked in advance. I used to wait and see when was best for clients for me to take time off. Believe me when they no longer need your services they will stop coming. It is not personal. The same as if we take a holiday at an inconvenient time for a client, it is not personal to them. It is just timing.

If you do not plan and book that holiday, time will pass, clients will book, and your holiday will not happen. Make you and your whys a priority.

Another big one is social media. Obviously, we use it for work, and I am often online and then I find myself saying I am just doing this, because... Andy says 'there is always something' and he is right.

He is very good at helping me with boundaries. When I am consumed by social media, I lose my own creative flair because I am consumed by what is going on outside my life. This is not great. If you are a Beauty Business Owner, you need to be on the ball and full of ideas.

We must make a choice. If we decide to do one thing, it means we have decided not to do another. By that I mean, how often do you feel you have not got time? What have you thought of lately, for work, and then not done it, because you did not have time? Yet you were spending an hour on Facebook or Instagram and not actually 'for work'.

Does this make sense?

It is about setting priorities and being clear and focused on what you want to do. Think about it. What could you have been doing instead of an hour on Facebook at lunch time?

Another good one, is not taking your phone to bed or not looking at it first thing. When we look at it first thing, we have not prioritised our needs, because we have already started to look at what the rest of the world is doing and that starts to quickly invade our mood.

Think about yours, be very specific, but do not feel overwhelmed. Hopefully I have given you lots of examples.

Start to put things in place, boundaries are life changing but stick to them. You have every right!

Decide to make some changes and put firm boundaries in place. You do not have to do many, just make a start. Try saying 'no' a few times. It will feel strange, and this will show how much you say yes, even when you do not want to.

Make sure you join my free 'Creating Salon Success' Facebook group and share with us your boundaries. Put it out into the world to commit to them.

Warren Buffet says, 'really successful people say no to everything!'. Respect other people's boundaries and they will respect yours...

This chapter turned out a little longer than I thought it would but I hope you can start to see how important boundaries are.

This is especially important when it comes to clients. If not we let them rule our lives. Even though they mean so much to us. We still must put ourselves first. Think back to your whys, your goals and what you want for you out of your life.

IT IS NOT PERSONAL

Beauty Therapy and being a Salon Owner, I believe, can be one of the worst jobs for things feeling personal. Being a therapist can often be looked on as a really glamourous and special job, and it can be. However, I do think it is a job that you need quite broad shoulders for as well. Let me explain...

Clients will happily tell you what they think, especially if they are not happy. This sounds awful but at least you get feedback and can make efforts to put things right. I always see this as the best way to help your customer service skills.

This is the way I would rather it go to be honest. I have built my whole business on people coming back and telling me they are not happy. That does not sound good. But I do not mean it as a negative. I have made sure my clients are comfortable enough to come back and tell me if they are not happy.

You may wonder why? I would much rather them be telling me than the person down the road or going to another salon and telling them how they were not happy at mine. Plus, it is how you deal with a complaint that can make a client for life or not.

It is hard to take at times, but I pride myself on my clients being happy and knowing they can come and talk to me. Maybe that could explain why my clients are more like friends now and some have been with me for 20 years. Now, I am not saying I have always got this right. Sometimes I have missed things. I know about 5 years ago when I was changing things up in my business and I was stepping back more and more, I remember a client telling me she wasn't happy with her nails. I had always done them but had not for the past year or so.

I would rectify and then she was happy. I then thought she was happy moving forward. I noticed she stopped coming. I messaged her and no response. I really missed seeing her. At first, I was upset and hurt, but then I realised I had taken my eye off the ball.

This is rare for me, but I was so focused on transitioning my business that I did not realise until a few months had gone by. By then she had found somewhere else. I cannot argue because she did try to tell me. I just was not listening. Not intentionally and I am mortified, however I have to take my error on the chin.

We still speak and when my cat died, she bought me a beautiful gift and I am so grateful that I have not lost her as a friend more than as a client. Like I said they are like friends to me and I would never intentionally hurt a friend.

Another reason I feel like this option is worse, is because clients can go elsewhere. No reason, no explanation (not that they should give one, by the way).

It always feels like it is those clients you have bent over backwards for and squeezed in at the drop of a hat when you know you should have said no. But do not forget clients have the right to spend money wherever they choose, as do we all.

Try not to focus on it. Move on and keep going. You can always ring them and really put your customer service skills to the test. You are more highly thought of and at least you tried, right? Being a Business Owner is often stepping out of your comfort zone and this is a fine way to do it.

I understand how hurtful it can feel; however, we have to accept it, move on. Without being rude, there is always another client. We just have to stay strong.

Please do not misunderstand me, it is always good to make attempts to find out if there was anything wrong and there is no harm in trying to get them back by doing a returning client offer. If they do not accept then it is time to move on.

We can sometimes get a bit of a bad reputation to clients when they see us stood at reception waiting for our next client. They deem it as you CAN fit them in for their quick eyebrow wax, yet you are not set up or anything.

Of course, we cannot fit them in. Your next client is due any moment and the bed is made and set for the treatment booked in. If we take that eyebrow shape in it can set us back at least 20 minutes, and that was before COVID.

We do need to give clients a break sometimes. They do not see what goes off behind the scenes in the salon and it is our job to hide that from them.

YOU CAN'T BUILD A BUSINESS ON FRIENDS/FAMILY

This chapter is not about friends working together. More a case of when friends and family try to give opinions on your business or when friends come for treatments. Or sometimes you can feel upset because friends go elsewhere and do not come to you for their appointments.

Stay strong in your goals and what YOU want out of your business.

Friends do not have to come to your salon

When friends go elsewhere it can leave you feeling like poo or like you are not good at your job. It will always be the ones you fitted in and have given a discount to or maybe even stayed late for. Then for whatever reason they go elsewhere. They never tell you why and then start telling you how wonderful such and such's salon is.

Do you ever think to yourself 'are you actually telling me all of this to make me feel like rubbish on purpose?' At this point they do not feel like great friends do they? I want to tell you now they do not even know they do it. It could almost be laughable if it did not feel so unkind.

I know I have felt that friends only come to me for convenience or the discount and not necessarily because they think I am good at my job. But just because they don't come it does not make you bad at your job either.

To be honest, I would rather friends and family did not come to my salon. You probably wonder why. There is often a discount given, so it takes the place of a full paying customer. I often feel rushed, because I am trying to fit them in for more than I have time for, because I do not want to upset them.

Then when they decide not to come to you or you really cannot fit them in they go elsewhere and pay full price anyway. But for some reason they do not want to pay you full price. It is baffling. But this explains the title of this chapter. You really cannot build a business on friends and family. If you do not give discount and treat them exactly like you would another client then of course you can. I am not telling you not to have friends and family in your salon, I am just saying not to give discounted prices.

Giving Beauty advice

Friends and family can often take up too much time out of work too, because they may be asking you lots of questions. This could be on a night out or even when you are relaxing watching TV and your phone keeps buzzing with questions.

You know how frustrating it can be when clients do not listen to your advice? I think it is even worse when a friend doesn't listen. Why ask?

I once did a treatment for a friend. It was something I knew worked, but it is not a cheap treatment. The training was not cheap and neither is the equipment.

It also uses consumables, so you cannot do it for free. But I stupidly still discounted the treatment, so much so I made no money.

My fault completely, but I wanted to help my friend. This is what I mean when I say I would rather they did not come, because I would not have a viable business.

I did the treatment and she was over the moon. I did tell her one treatment would not be enough. However, she told me she was really happy. I cannot tell you how pleased that made me feel.

She never came for the rest doing and she told me it was too expensive. I felt a little hurt as I gave her the treatment basically at cost price. But do I have a right to feel hurt? Like I said, it is never personal. But you are only human after all.

One evening this same person spent ages messaging me asking about different things she could buy. I just thought by the time she had finished purchasing, she may as well have come in the salon for the treatment. It is crazy how people think, but that is their prerogative.

I was hurt that my advice did not seem to be taken seriously or as if it was not valid. But is that my friends' fault or mine?

Nobody's really, but it is my responsibility to not take things so personal and have boundaries in place.
It is my responsibility I do not waste my time out of working giving advice that may not be listened to.

Friends often tell me how someone has given this advice or that advice to the point where I just decided to stop advising or saying anything. I am not a fan of wasting energy and I felt like my advice and opinions were not valued anyway.

I know I am not alone here and the reason I am sharing is it happens all the time. It does not bother me now, but it does not stop me from wanting to stand and scream and say I have been doing this for 20 years.

I pride myself on making a difference and helping people feel good. So why won't you listen to me?

I realise, it is not about me, it is about them. When people do not listen, it makes you feel rubbish and so low and this is why you cannot take it personally and why you need broad shoulders.

Yes, it is frustrating, but you cannot dwell on it. My advice is to concentrate on those people/clients who do value your opinions and advice. These are the people who will make your business. Do not spend time focusing on friends and family.

They do not mean to devalue your expertise; they just see you as their friend. Maybe they do not feel like they are your friend at this point. But what I am saying is you have to take yourself out of the situation. It is not personal, and this is why you should not do discounts for friends and family.

I make an exception for my Mum because she does so much for me. But you know what I mean, give discounts wisely.

Do not give discount easily

You have a business to run and those who ask or expect discounts are not really valuing your services. Just keep that in mind.

You are now a Business Person and you must behave like you are and then people will treat you like so. Just like your boundaries.

Someone once said to me:

'You cannot build a business based on friends and family. It is when others start coming and friends and family do not that you have really made a business'.

The other thing I once heard is:

'A friend will go somewhere else and pay £2 for a bottle of water rather than pay you £1, because you would not give her a discount.'

Of course, this is not always the case. I am just sharing some things I have heard. One thing I do not like is when you feel a little bit used and this is why I share these points with you as I do not want you to feel used.

As you can imagine I have a 100 stories like these, as I am sure you do too. You have to concentrate on us and our business. I know I have said this a lot!!

Being in business can feel like you are fighting against people all the time. Friends and family will all have their opinion on how you should run your business. Often their ideas will not work because they have not been there and done it.

Making changes

You run the risk of upsetting people when you make changes to your business and this can include clients too. This is because they do become more like friends.

Many do not like change. But you have your goals for what you want your business to look like. Stay focused on them.

Being in business often means things need to change in order to progress or make things more efficient. Especially if you are a one-man band.

You cannot be everything all the time and make a profit too. You still need that work life balance.

An example of a big change you could be making is introducing a booking system.
From personal experience I know this can cause a few feelings of upset because people like you to book them in.

I am sure there is an element where you like to take control and book them in too, I know I did.

But you cannot split ourselves in 10 and be everything to everyone and do everything needed in running a successful Beauty Salon either. You have to think of ways you can save ourselves time and be more efficient.

Believe me it takes far less time, just to check people have booked correctly online, than it does to ring them back and book them in. Of course, if you need to adapt the online booking, you can, and it will take minutes.

If you are trying to step back from your business and let staff manage a bit more or if you are introducing new staff, or even stopping certain treatments it can cause upset. My advice is stay focused.

This is hard and it is where a coach can really help. When you try to speak to family and friends about business they cannot help but see it more from a client point of view more than a business point of view.

You are the one working in your business. You know your dreams and goals and therefore it is you who can make them happen.

Other people's input can often change your path. As Beauty Therapists, I think you can be programmed to be a 'people pleaser' and you will do this naturally.

If someone disagrees with us it is easy to think they are correct. There is no right or wrong.

Just stay focused on your business dream and your vision for your future with your family. If the changes you want to make will bring you closer to your long-term goal, then that is what you need to do.

Believe me when I say, everyone else is focused on their goals and their needs, so make sure you are too. Please do not think you are wrong for this.

DREAMS AND VISIONS

Those in my Creating Salon Success group know I often speak about dreams and visualisation.

Dreams help us create goals and help us have an amazing business.

If you do not know what you want out of life, how can you make it happen? By this I mean, you do not have to settle for 'a secure job'. Society has often dictated to us how you 'should' live.

People have often said to me, 'you need to settle down Louisa' or 'no man will want you when you are so flighty'. I did not understand what they meant at the time.

I do now, however I am grateful I did not get it because I think I would have felt pressured to settle down and do what you 'should do'. That is just not me.

From the outside, I know many people who have said about me and not always to me:

'she is never happy'. 'She always wants the next thing', 'she will never settle', 'she is chasing something that does not exist' or 'will she ever settle in a job?'

Clients often say to me, 'Louisa the salon is always different. You can't settle'. I can, I just have a dream and it is not there yet.

10 years ago, I was selling the property where my salon was based. I wanted to move to Australia and while that dream has not happened yet, it is still there.

Anyway, at the same time there was another building in Aston (my village) that came up for sale. I used to drive past it on my way home, every day.

Every day I used to look at that for sale sign and think, 'Gosh I wish I could have that building. I would have really made it. How incredible would that be?'.

That building was 6 times the price of my current property and I just saw it as a pipe dream.

It used to make me smile though. It was such an amazing building. It was in the posh bit of Aston, big and just looked so impressive. Nothing wrong with dreaming.

Anyway 10 years later, guess where I am? And to top it off after leasing it for years, guess what I bought? Yes... That same property.

I could cry (happy tears of course) when I look back. I NEVER imagined this would be possible.

This is what I am saying. It was a pipe dream. But now it is real.

Dreams are something adults can find difficult. Whenever I discuss this topic in workshops, I am often met with blank faces or stressed faces.

It is as if you stop dreaming or life drums it out of us. I remember in art at school being asked to draw a dream. I said I do not dream at night.

Looking back, he meant draw a dream of something you visualise, a pipe dream for your own existence. I could have drawn a castle at the side of a beach.

That would make sense to me now. But back then I just did not get it and it caused me so much stress. Crazy I know. I must have been 13 years old at the time and the idea to dream was already drilled out of me.

As an adult and Business Owner I have educated myself so much and I have learnt to dream again. It is not silly or childish. Yes, it may be unrealistic, but hey, *if you do not have a dream, how can you have a dream come true?* I love this saying.

Ok, so what do I mean by dream? It is the way you would love your life to look, yet it seems like a pipe dream.

It is so important to have these kinds of dreams and to visualise your life of how you would love it to be.

No matter how old you are dreams are important. They encompass goals and so much more.
They give your life purpose, direction, and meaning. Sounds crazy, doesn't it?

However, they shape your life choices, help you build toward the future, and give you a sense of control and hope. I know so many people (including myself), who forget about their hopes and dreams.

So many of our dreams at first seem impossible, then they seem improbable, and then, when you summon the will, they soon become inevitable.

> 'If you talk about it, it's a dream, if you envision it, it's possible, but if you schedule it, it's real.'
> - Tony Robbins

A dream is an expression of your potential and gives voice to what could be.

Remember those famous words from Martin Luther King, Jr., 'I have a dream!'

Dreamers are the ones who have the courage and creativity to see beyond 'what is' to 'what can be' to make a difference in their own life and the lives of others.

Do you ever find at the beginning of a new year you feel it is a fresh start? A time to build on what you have already learned and get past any challenges you faced during the last year.

You may not realise, but it all starts with a dream.

You know when you have an idea on how you are going to change your salon?

These changes will generate this much income and you will be able to now achieve this or that.

This is a dream, a start anyway. Then you visualise that dream and make it your reality!!

You can often put limitations on our dreams, because as an adult you can assess whether something is 'realistic' or not.

Remember, there are NO limitations to your dreams and visions, only the ones you set yourself so bring out that mindset of a child and dream BIG!

Imprint your dreams into your subconscious mind.

'Destiny is determined by the choices you make. Choose now, choose well' – Tony Robbins

Dream big and stretch your mind to envisage what is possible. This is my favourite part of being in business.

The freedom to dream and visualise and then plan and create. It is so exciting!

Opportunity does not come and find you. You have to go out there and find IT. The worst thing you can do is nothing. Do not over analyse.

This can make you feel stuck. By this I mean as if you are stuck between reality and your dreamworld.

Finding out what makes you tick is a great place to start.
I have put together some questions. I would like you to answer them as if you are already doing them.

I know the words 'it is not realistic' will kick in here as I hear this all the time when I am doing workshops.

Please remember this is pretend. Try and let your mind run free into a crazy fantasy world. Enjoy it!

You are practicing dreaming here but you are visualising it too. Let go of any control.

Please do not answer with a 'what you would be happy with', answer.

Answer with something beyond your wildest dreams. Ignite your imagination!!

- What is your dream business like?
- Where in the world do you live?
- What is your dream home? Style? Country? City Beach? Village? Quaint? Modern?
- How many hours a week do you work in your salon?
- What is your dream salon? Style of property? Colours?
- How many customers do you want and by when?
- How much money do you want to make and by when? No limitations. Why don't you want a million?
- What does your dream day look like? How does it start? How does it end? And what happens in between?
- How do you see your life?
- Who inspires you? - Great things happen when you feel inspired

Dreams are what you need to know about yourself. Release them and start to visualise them in your mind.

Spend a few minutes each day, dreaming about how you would love things to look or be.

It does not mean you are not happy with how things are, it just means you have a plan for your future life. Create a vision board and put your dreams up there for you to see every day.

Visualisation can take time, so don't give yourself a hard time. It is about reinforcing the dreams in our minds!

NO NEED TO BE RUDE

I bet you wonder what this chapter is about. Well, I feel that clients can sometimes overstep. This is confirmation as to why you need boundaries in place, why you need broad shoulders and why it is important to stay focused on your goals and your why.

Would you ever insult your client? Would you ever ask them why they are so fat? Or comment unprofessionally about their acne? I already know the answer! Of course, you would not. Obviously, you would have no clients for a start. But it is also just downright rude.

Do you ever have clients comment on your life, behaviour, or your image? I know I have.

Remember, I told you about my stress and IBS and how horrible I felt? Well at this time I would have numerous clients often tell me I was too skinny. If you comment on how fat someone is, it is so wrong. However, is it ok to comment just because someone is thin?

It wasn't just one client, either. It was constant. I just smiled and carried on. However, each time I heard this, I don't think I realised it was chipping away at my self-worth. But I was allowing it to happen. Clearly, I had no boundaries and just accepted it. What I am saying is, something that starts with a shrug of the shoulders and an 'oh well whatever' attitude, should often be nipped in the bud straight away. Over time, it is almost a form of bullying. I know this is never someone's intention and anyone reading this may think 'oh goodness I said that to her'.

I do not blame anyone. It is a learning curve, and I am sharing this with you, to remind you to put your boundaries in place. It is almost laughable that you give clients such power over us.

Like I said, nobody knew what I was going through. I did not really comprehend it myself, yet people would poke fun or make comments. I just used to smile and half laugh, but inside I thought 'if only you knew'. I try not to make comment on people's weight and other personal things, because you just never know what is going off.

Hilariously, would you believe, that once I started to put on a bit of weight when I was getting better clients then started making comments again!

It would be in forms of things like 'Ooh Louisa, there is quite a bit more of you now!'. It was not said in a nice way and bear in mind I was still probably no more than 8 stone. But as usual I just took it on the chin, whilst thinking people can be so mean and unfair.

Well, I actually thought 'Oh my goodness, I am too thin, I am now getting fat. When will you all be happy?'. Of course, it was nothing to do with me really and nor did my being fat or thin make them happy. People just love to comment. I do not believe any harm or malice is meant. But that is why you have to be in control of our own feelings and boundaries.

People even commented on my husband. Someone once saw my husband and they said, 'ooh Louisa, I didn't expect you to be with someone like that'. I was instantly offended and asked what did they mean? She replied 'well, bald and tattoos'.

Wow, how judgemental. My husband is a soft as a brush. Do not cross him of course, but that is nothing to do with tattoos or being bald. That is because he will not accept anybody's rubbish, nor will he allow people to treat him in a negative way or disrespect his boundaries. Gosh I could learn a thing or two from him, that is for sure.

Tattoos are a choice, that does not make someone's personality. I do not have any, it does not make me nice or not nice. And being bald is not something you have much control over, is it? However, your judgement is totally in your control!

If only she knew I only began to get better when Andy came into my life. She was judging him and yet he was my rescuer.

Dramatic, I know, but that is how I see it.

I will be forever grateful to him. I do not share that with him though. You have to keep somethings to ourselves, right? I joke here of course.

Another occasion, where I feel the client completely overstepped is on an occasion when a client said I was 'ugly'.

For me this is so rude and you do not say this about people. Everyone is entitled to an opinion, of course. However, imagine saying this about a client and what kind of reputation would you salon have then?

You may be wondering how this occurred. Well, when I worked above a hairdressers, it was amazing what I could hear upstairs. I heard this client saying 'ooh whatever you do, don't have your hair like her upstairs'

Hairdresser: 'Why don't you like it'

Client: 'I don't. I mean it is not like she is pretty is it? If she was, she may be able to pull it off'

Hairdresser: Don't you think?

Client: I do not! She is ugly!

Little did anyone realise I was coming downstairs at this point. I could hear and thought 'there is no way that is about me, because that is so rude'. You cannot help what you are born with, after all.
When I got to the bottom of the stairs, I just said 'hi'. Faces were a picture. So, if I doubted, they were talking about me, their faces confirmed they were.

I asked one of the hairdressers if I had heard correctly. He said 'yes, your hair is awful and you are butt ugly'. He laughed and said, 'don't worry, babe, we know it is not true!' I get that and I agree. However, it is just rude!!

The lady refused to apologise and said she could think what she wanted and she is right. I just do not think it is very nice and I think very unnecessary and unkind.

A few weeks went by, and I bumped into her coming out of the toilet. I was not scared to bump into her, however I had been avoiding her. This was an occasion my mask would not be enough!

However, she said 'Louisa, can I have a word'. I politely went to her and she said 'I want to apologise for the other week'. I said 'ok'.

I do not know about you I would expect the next word to be sorry. No, it was:

'Do you know anyone who wants to buy a microwave!!?'

Crazy, right?

It made me think she was bonkers and I cannot help but really laugh about this situation now.

There was no real apology and that was fine. But it just makes you think, doesn't it?

I had been nothing but nice to this woman. Why would someone be so rude? But I guess that is just people for you.

I was more annoyed than upset by it because I just found it so rude and unkind. However, I have no control over her or anyone else for that matter. It is hard, but this is how you have to think.

These are just a couple of examples, and I am sure you have soooo many of your own. I have plenty more, but I wanted to share to reinforce the need for boundaries. I want to remind you that just because you provide a service, does not mean you have to accept everything that is thrown at us.

You are human too!

Remember, you do not have to accept every customer that walks through your door.

Put it out to the universe for what customers you want and you will get them. Visualise them and do not accept anything less.

MOTIVATION

It is so easy to lose momentum and motivation when running a salon. It is often seen as a glamourous and beautiful industry, and it is. However, business of any kind can be tough, and you get knocked down time and time again. But it is these knocks that build our strength and build our knowledge and character too.

The term motivation is frequently used to describe why a person does something. It is the driving force behind human actions. Once again, it all links back to aligning our goals, dreams, and our reasons for being (your why), then motivation comes.

Motivating ourselves can be hard and it takes time and effort. To motivate is internal, rather than external and a challenge for almost every Business Owner.

Without motivation you can fall short of reaching important goals. It is hard and motivation is key for us to stay focused. How many times have you felt you have lost motivation?

This is where being surrounded by like-minded people can help. People are social creatures, and knowing who you are, deep down and your passions and your dreams; it is essential you discover individuals who align with your qualities and your beliefs.

It is often said, you can tell a lot about a person by the company they keep. Pay attention. It is safe to say that they are either pushing you forward or keeping you down.

Get involved in a community of salon owners, like the Creating Salon Success group I run. I love the support in that group. Motivation is not something that can be done for you. But you can do things that make you feel inspired and which can help create that drive you need.

Love plays a big part and when you give love for things, you cannot help but be grateful for everything around us. When you feel gratitude and love, it is hard to feel negative emotions. This can help us stay motivated to achieve more and make our lives and businesses a big success.

For those who know me, I often talk about a book by Rhonda Byrnes called 'The Power'. This is all about giving love for things and being grateful. It is extremely powerful and incredibly life changing. However, this requires daily reinforcing.

Doing what you love gives us reason and gives us purpose. If you do not feel love for what you do, you will rapidly become demotivated.

How frequently have you doubted why you should be on this planet? How frequently have you doubted your actual presence? I am guessing, numerous times.

Our character is an impression of what you are willing to accept. However, our feeling of character can be undermined by outside factors. This can lead to an enormous amount of pressure.

If you or your staff are unmotivated it can negatively affect your salon and your life.

Staff members can often mirror the attitudes and behaviour of senior workers. This could even be you. I understand the pressure of being a Business Owner.

Let us look at what are the demotivating factors:

- Unfair/negative/public criticism.
- Feeling under-appreciated
- Failure or fear of failure.
- Boredom
- Unmanageable workload
- Unsuitable working environment
- Lack of career progression
- Issues outside of work such as family illness, bereavement, or financial worries

Being a Business Owner and Beauty Therapist can be difficult because life still goes on around us. Even when we have personal issues, we have to carry on. If we do not, then our business could fold.

This is an enormous amount of pressure and why we need such a healthy mindset.

Look out for any changes in both staff and your behaviour or attitude. It can be difficult to recognise it in yourself as it can just creep up.
A lack of motivation can be expressed as a lack of interest in things, withdrawal or diminished activity.

Can you think back to a time you have felt like this? Or is it something you are currently feeling? Do not despair. It is not just you. We can all feel this way from time to time. Business is hard and sometimes it just all gets on top of us!

Whenever I feel demotivated. I realise it is often because I have too much going on in my life and I am starting to feel slightly overwhelmed. I am trying to do too much. I can also be concentrating on too many goals and I have lost focus.

This takes away my energy and motivation. It is probably the most common mistake that many Business Owners make, especially when they are trying to work both in the business and on the business.

Sometimes the balance is not quite right, and they try to take on too much. You cannot maintain energy and focus. Focusing on just one goal at a time can really help.

If you are trying to do two or more goals at once, it is virtually impossible. Choose one goal for now and focus on it completely.

If we prioritise our goals and fulfil one at a time we can do each one well. You can always do your other goals when you have accomplished your one goal.

It helps to be excited about your goals. Of course when you are not motivated this is difficult. Well, it starts with inspiration from others and taking that excitement and building on it.

For me, inspiration comes from looking at others who have achieved what I want to achieve, or who are currently doing it. I read blogs, listen to audio books, read books and magazines and watch You Tube videos.

I would never say routines are for me. However, I have learnt that routines can really help achieve success and, weirdly, routines help motivate you as well.

MORNING ROUTINES

What is that saying? It takes three weeks to form a habit. Carry this on for 90 days and it becomes routine.

You may be wondering what I mean?

Morning routines and evening routines can really motivate you. Some of the most successful people in history have relied on morning routines to help them start their day consistently. From the likes of Oprah Winfrey to Barack Obama, just to name a couple.

When you have a morning routine it has so many benefits. They are best planned and often begin at night. It is always best to be prepared.

A morning routine gives you a chance to start with positive momentum that will carry you through the rest of the day. It also gives you a chance to set your priorities. This allows you to focus on productive work that's most important to you.

Creating a morning routine gives you the control to start your day in the way you want to and to prioritise what you care about most.

If you don't, we end up letting other people, emails, and notifications interrupt your morning and this makes you start your day re-actively.

People often say 'I haven't got time for a morning routine'. This is why planning it is so important and getting our time management in control really helps.

There are some common aspects of a morning routine that can get you started and help you figure out what will work best for you. Obviously, the first part of your morning routine will be waking up.

But even if you are well-rested when you first wake up, you can still face sleep inertia. That's the groggy feeling you get just after waking up. This makes your eyes feel heavy and makes you feel like going back to sleep is the best thing to do.

Building elements into your morning routine to help you overcome sleep inertia more quickly can make it easier to wake up and get started with your day. Try the RISE UP approach, it can leave you feeling alert and awake just minutes after waking up:

Refrain from snoozing
Increase activity for the first hour
Shower or wash face
Expose yourself to sunlight
Upbeat music
Phone a friend; talking makes you feel good

Create your own positive morning routine by finding activities that make you smile to start your day with.

Exercise is what helps my mindset and I stand by this to start your day well. Exercise releases happy feelings. I am not saying you need to take up running, but a quick walk around the block would work! Find what works for you. Try a few ideas until you find the one that is right. You could even vary it up, Yoga one day and running the next and then walking the next. Do what's important to you.

Starting your day positively will help you control the feeling of your day. A morning routine can also help you find time to prioritise projects/tasks. One piece of advice I would give is avoid your phone first thing. I know the rise up says phone a friend but it is more about getting you talking. Talking can be motivating.

The purpose of the morning routine is to get one small win to create momentum in each life domain that's important to you.

Why not make a list of all the areas of your life you want to work on every day. This might include your own business or side projects, keeping in touch with friends and family, stretching your brain, or staying fit and healthy. Look back at the boundaries and values chapters. Remind yourself what is important to you.

For each area on the list, add one action to move it forward to your morning routine. This way, you'll start your day by working on the areas of your life that you care about most, setting the tone for your day.

Here is an example of a morning routine:

Best morning routine recipe

- Prepare to be productive
- Write your to do list the night before
- Get a good night's sleep
- Get up early
- Read/listen to audio
- Light exercise - to focus your mind
- Eat a good breakfast
- Start with the worst job

L.A ACADEMY
Creating salon success

Here are four ways to get you started on your own positive, productive morning routine:

- No snoozing and add a little exercise, just a few stretches to get your body moving.
- Clear your mind with writing – start journaling, just a few sentences, maybe list 3 things you are grateful for or 3 tasks you want to get done today.
- Start with positivity – gratitude and focus
- Take action towards your goals

Once you are up and running with your morning routine, you can adjust your routine based on your lifestyle, your goals.

Even make it flexible to account for times when you are busier.

With a little tweaking you can develop a personal morning routine to set you up with positive momentum to carry you throughout the rest of your day.

When you do this and do it regularly you will feel so much motivation and control for the day.

On the next page circle the answer most relevant to you. This helps you work out where you are the most productive and when you need to give yourself a break.

Question	A	B	C	D
What type of exercise works best for you?	A high-energy workout to kick-start the day	Beginning your day with Yoga or Pilates	A post-work fitness class	A late night run to clear your head
You have a busy week with extra work. You...	Wake up early and get a head start on the day's tasks.	Try and do a little before work and a little after.	Start again every evening to make up the time.	Keep working all night until the early hours.
Your ideal day would involve...	wake up early, run before breakfast, errands done before lunch.	sleep in an hour later than usual and go for brunch with friends.	a nice lie-in and a leisurely afternoon with friends.	sleep until 11ish and enjoy my evening into the night.
What does your meal-time schedule look like?	Breakfast at 7am, lunch at 12pm, dinner before 6pm.	Breakfast before 8am, lunch by 1pm and dinner around 7pm.	Breakfast by 9, lunch at 1/2pm and dinner before 8pm.	Breakfast 11, lunch never before 2 and dinner whenever.
If you have a creative task, when would you start it?	First thing, when I wake up early I have the most ideas.	11ish, once my day has started properly.	Late, my thoughts are more connected.	Late evening, into the night, my creativity comes alive.
Which do you choose to do with friends?	Take a sunrise hike	Have a catch up over brunch	Catch a late film showing	Drinks and dancing into the early hours
What's your sleep routine look like?	Bed by 10pm, ready for the next day.	Try to get 7 or 8 hours sleep a night.	Difficult before 12 – I function on less sleep.	Usually in bed by 12 but can be later.

RESULTS AND CREATING HABITS

As I have just been speaking about, morning routines can massively impact your day in an extremely positive way.

Did you answer the questions? Which did you circle the most of A, B, C or D's?

Here are the results, depending on where you scored:

Mostly A's - you love mornings. You're up early to work and have done a workout. You feel mornings are your time. You're early to bed and early to rise and you wouldn't have it any other way.
Mostly B's - you think mornings are pretty useful. You'll hit snooze every once in a while, but you're usually up and doing stuff early and feeling pretty productive.
Mostly C's - you're tired of mornings and tired of morning people. Who's really that enthusiastic before 10AM? Your only true friend in this world is the snooze button.
Mostly D's - you have never done a single productive thing before 1PM. That is OK too. Mornings are terrible and sleeping is the best thing in the whole world and that's just the way it's always going to be.
All the above are fabulous. There is no right or wrong, but it is extremely useful to work out where you are the most productive.

It helps you. This is why I decided to stop working ridiculously late at night. I love early nights and if I do not get it I am absolutely useless the next day. I just cannot function. Not to mention our jobs are tiring.

All I am doing here is pointing out you are who you are and helping you do what is best for you. You will find it all fits together in the end and you will wish you had done it sooner.

Not getting up early is as bad for me as not going to bed early enough or not getting enough sleep. I am not saying I have to be in bed at 8pm. I can still be the last one dancing at a party. However, my optimum time with work and general living is mornings. 6-6.30 is my ideal time of getting up and I love a good stomp/sometimes run around my local lake or a swim at my local swimming baths.

However, sometimes I much prefer yoga in the house. I love getting up before everyone else. Before the world wakens. That is what I feel like when I am up, that the world has not got going yet. It really feels like MY time.

This feeling is extremely empowering. However, I am not saying that you have to get up early to have a successful day or feel empowered. I do recommend finding a routine that works for you though. Even if you get up at 9 and with your eyes closed do a few stretches I would recommend it. It wakes your body. I chat about morning and evening routines a lot in my group.

I hear, all the time, I do not have time for a morning routine. It does not have to be complicated or even take up that much time. Please do what works for you. Just find something that motivates and invigorates you. There is so much at our fingertips, it is just sometimes finding the thing that works for you.

If you haven't yet, please have a look at the questions and see where you fit and look at my example of a routine. You can make it as short or as long as you like.

This morning, before I started my work, I had a cup of tea and gathered my thoughts in peace. I did 15 minutes of yoga with Adriene, followed by 15 minutes of Kundalini Yoga.

You DO NOT have to do 30 mins, but 15 minutes could be easy to find, do you think?

Imagine waking up 20 minutes earlier and just starting your day in pure bliss and harmony. For me, this feeling is worth getting out of bed earlier.

Let me tell you a little about Kundalini Yoga.

Firstly, it feels like the weirdest and craziest thing to do. However, once you get past feeling a bit weird you will feel the amazing benefits Kundalini offers.

Kundalini is an ancient Sanskrit word that literally means coiled snake. In early Eastern religion it was believed that each individual possessed a divine energy at the base of the spine.

This energy was thought to be the sacred energy of creation and it is something we are born with, but we must make an effort to uncoil the snake.

Kundalini Yoga is the practice of awakening our Higher Self and turning potential energy into kinetic energy. This energy literally feels like waves of ecstasy. Do not get me wrong, Kundalini is not easy. It is quite tiring, and you know you have done it. But it feels soooo good.

Sounds crazy, I know. It is a combination of both physical exercise and meditation, it activates the energy centres within the body. These centres are usually referred to as your chakras. It is almost like exercise with a touch of spiritual enlightenment.

If you haven't tried it, I highly recommend a 15 minute Kundalini session, free on YouTube and then feedback how amazing you feel. Working on our inner peace and inner harmony is crucial when we are running a business, a household and enjoying our life all at the same time.

I understand that when you have done your session, life will resume and that peace and harmony you have created will disperse until the next time. However, the more you practice it the more the feeling lasts.

Plus, when you are calm inside it can help you deal and manage situations better.

Take this morning, for example, I had a beautiful morning and then I wondered where my cat was. He is an indoor cat, however, has an outdoor area. I lost him, which in itself stresses me thinking he has escaped and I worry for his safety.

But do you know where I found him? On top of his outdoor area in the most bizarre place and then he is meowing at me as if it is my fault.

This does not sound stressful but you know when you have lost something and you are running around wanting to find it? That feeling but with your fur baby is big. However, the point is, I stayed calm. Well calmer than I normally would have anyway.

IDEAL CLIENT

I am sure you have heard these words many times before. You may wonder how important this is. I agree. I have always struggled with this. However, you know when you get it and it clicks, it changes everything.

It makes your marketing easier, your social media strategies simple and all in all people understand you, and your vision for your business.

Yes, of course everyone is welcome in your salon, I know. This is exactly what I used to say. However, when you attract the right clients into your salon, your business is a much nicer and much easier place to work.

People buy into your values. This includes your business values. If you share your beliefs and values, you attract the right customer for you and your salon. When you are clear on your business vision and mission it all starts to fall into place.

You may be wondering what is your ideal customer? This is different for every salon and everyone. I know there are the common charts you will find online. I have used them myself. However, for our industry, I am not always sure these are the best way to work it out.

Our ideal customer can massively vary in age, job, the car they drive and their values. When you have the 'easiest' or 'best' clients in look at what is the same about them all.

Often, you will find it is more their ethics and values that you need to look at.

A quick way to find your ideal client is by looking at you! Sounds bonkers, doesn't it?

Those who share your beliefs will want to come to your salon. For example, I have really condensed my price list instead of being everything to everyone, which is not sustainable long term nor is it pleasurable for you. My passion has never been nails, yet I fell into the trap of just doing them to keep everyone happy and not upset the apple cart.

Now I have created, built and more importantly spent money on a spa area. This was my passion, inner wellbeing. I am all about holistically looking after you. Nails and lashes and makeup have their place in the industry and there are some very talented therapists doing those treatments too. However, it is not for me. I decided to make an extremely scary statement and say my salon is no longer providing nails as a service.

Bold move, right?

This was scary; however, I knew in my heart it was the right move and the best move for me.

It was the only way I could move my business in the direction I wanted it to go in.

I was becoming really unhappy again. I had already stopped doing nails but when one of my staff went on maternity, I covered for her. It was nice, but not fulfilling for me.

I am grateful and will also treasure my clients who had their nails done with me, but I had to stop. Plus, I became really allergic too and nothing about nails was pleasurable for me.

Anyway, not to dwell. What I am saying is look at the direction you want your business to go in. People now come from all over the country to my spa.

The feeling of elation I get from this is incredible and makes business worthwhile again.

Does this make sense? Do you feel you could be this bold? Sometimes it is the only way!!

When you have your ideal client nailed and you know exactly who you want to attract, things become streamlined.

Do not be fooled into thinking they must earn x amount of money, or they must drive this car. Many people who are willing to spend the money with your salon may not fit that criteria.

For example I am attracting clients who need some time out and they want the feeling of inner calm and peace. They want the harmony back in their lives and they need time out to recharge.

This is the place I have created for them, and it works.

Everything is so much more fulfilling and job satisfaction is 100% there.

I am not saying you cannot keep that really loyal client who you have done for 10 years on as nails. It is more about where you advertise and what new clients you are bringing in. Do not waste your time in an area that is not giving you what you want or need.

Remember I said be the expert in what you do? Create a niche and share your passions and that is the client you will attract.

You create your business so make it your dream creation!

Being selfish is not a bad thing, it is the key to being happy.

Just remember you cannot please everyone all of the time and trying to is a recipe for stress and misery. You are not responsible for how somebody feels only for how YOU feel.

Just because you can, it does not mean you should.

Try pleasing yourself and be happy, you may be surprised how this actually enables you to make others happy and feel good.

STAFF MANAGEMENT

Relationships are so important as staff can literally run rings around you. It is hard to stay professional, as usually you work in such close proximity that the relationships can become more personal.

This is lovely, however it is often also a mistake. It is a shame, especially when you get on well and you really like your staff. However, the problem is when discipline needs to be shown, it can be taken personally on the other side.

As the boss/owner, it is your responsibility to ensure boundaries are kept. Staff often feel entitled to certain things, whether that be a pay rise, time off when they want or they are just not happy with things.

As a Salon Owner, the job you loved (Beauty Therapy) becomes the last thing you do and now you find yourself in some sort of HR role, which you never wanted. You end up dealing with petty squabbles within the team and all issues that may arise.

If a staff member is not performing, you have action plans to sort. The job you had and loved and gone self-employed for is now no more! You are now a Business Owner, which is fantastic and you just have to accept how the role plays out.

I am actually very lucky with my current team of staff, however, as mentioned there have been many issues. And if I decided to go further back, I could go on and on with stories of thieving and more sense of entitlement. But stories can just become boring as it is just what can happen when you have to manage people.

One I will mention briefly, though, is what can happen when business and personal mix in a complicated way. I am not saying this is something that can be nipped in the bud, as you cannot control people.

I once lost an amazing staff member. She had worked with me since her work experience from college.

I had moulded her to my way of working and she could run my salon with her eyes closed. Clients loved her too, which is a massive plus. You know how picky people can be and rightly so too.

Getting staff is one of the most rewarding yet the most stressful things ever, too. Finding the right person, for both the salon ethics, clients and for you can be hard.

This staff member had worked for me for 12 years. She had met my brother-in-law many times, from my wedding back in 2006, to my 30th in 2010 and a few other occasions.

For some reason back in 2014 their eyes seemed to meet across my salon and before you know it, they are dating.

All was well and I loved having them together because they are both fantastic people.

Of course, it was all great, until it was not!

I made the mistake of trying to support the staff member, showing I was there for them and always trying to keep personal life out of it. This really did not work, and it was never going to!

After just a few months, our working relationship fell apart too. I felt very sad about this, yet really it was inevitable. I tried not to cause any more stress to her and kept a lot of my own issues from her. They were in a professional capacity.

For example, there was a lot of ringing in unable to come to work and I did not reprimand or make an issue.

This in itself was causing me so much stress. Every time she was due in it seemed like there would be a drama. My anxiety was through the roof at this point and I realised this was not healthy for me.

I did not want to add to her burden and be the boss from hell but I was taking all of this on my shoulders, which was a bit unfair.

But because I was very much aware of what was happening in her life I felt like I should minimise her burden as she had a lot going off.

Without being rude, this was not my doing and not my fault. It was as if I was trying to rectify a situation. Of course I could not.

Once again, I had put someone else's needs above my own and I did not address things that needed to be addressed, because I did not want to upset the apple cart.

When their relationship fell apart it had a very negative effect on our relationship, which was such a shame as I classed her as a friend too. Again, boundaries were much needed here.

I am quite good at separating business and friendship; however, this was hard because I was stuck in the middle of family, business and a friend.

Anyway, this all led into my relationship with her breaking down, in both a work capacity and personal. Such a shame. Obviously, there was little I could do to change things. However, I do miss her in the salon.

Her priorities had changed too and rightly so. There are no hard feelings. It just makes me sad as we always had a great relationship personally and business wise. This is just an example of how things can change.

However, it has taken me 15 years to get a team of staff I can trust and work well with. We have an amazing team. This I am eternally grateful for.

GIVE YOURSELF A BREAK

This is half a funny story and half not.

No doom and gloom here but back in 2019 my Mum got diagnosed with colon cancer. It was the worst news I could have ever heard. I was so broken, and I knew I had to be strong for everyone, but I could not find it in me for a while.

I constantly cried. I could not speak to people and it was the worst feeling I have ever had. Fast forward and I am grateful to report she is absolutely fine now.

Anyway, they were able to operate, but at this time we had no clue how bad it was and if she would be ok. She is far from old but she is no spring chicken either. Any operation is scary without chopping out your bowel and then adding the word cancer in too.

I could have quite happily taken all this time off work. But I did not want to let staff or clients down and really what would I do? I wanted to spend all the time with my Mum but did not want to smother her either.

This was so hard to get the balance and then face customers. I do think our job is one of the hardest when you have personal things going on. Do not get me wrong, any customer facing role is, I know that. But, also putting the effort into a treatment when you are not feeling your best makes things harder too.

Back to the story...

I had worked until late on a particular Wednesday evening. I was completely drained, and I had stopped working Thursdays, but I decided to go in.

Every bit of me thought about ringing my client to come on the Wednesday evening and stay later. But I was tired and thought 'no it will be ok', I will come Thursday. A good night's sleep will do me good.

However, there was no good night's sleep and by the time Thursday came, I was so tired and drained. Oops I knew this was a mistake, but I did not want to let anyone down.

My client came and she is someone I get on really well with. One of my favourite clients, so everything was wonderful.

I told her I had thought about ringing her to come Wednesday and she said 'oh I wish you had!'

First realisation moment!

I was doing her a pedicure. I felt really out of sorts and little did I know my client was exhausted too. She is a nurse and works some number of hours.

This was a couple of days after my Mum had been for her operation and I was desperate to go and see her again, whilst also filled with worry too. I did not even tell my lovely client about my Mum as I did not want to be 'woe is me' or doom and gloom.

Anyway, my client was a little fidgety and I was all over the place too.

This is in no way me passing the buck I am trying to explain as this does not show me in a good light, nor as a good therapist. But I am sharing with you because we must listen to our bodies.

Ok, I was doing her feet and I love to scrape dead skin off. All my clients and staff know it is my favourite bit. And then to my absolute horror, blood was sat in my hand and pouring out of my client's foot. I may be being slightly dramatic here, but I kid you not I was beyond mortified.

I take such pride in my job and believe me this kind of thing does not happen to me. I have made more mistakes than I care to mention, but I have learnt from them and always do a good job. I believe this is why clients come back and often ask for me to do their treatments. Which is an honour.

I digress again...

Ok, I told her what I had done and if you did not get the gist, I scraped too much and took a layer of skin off.

Well, if you have ever had a cut on your hands or feet the bleeding is hard to stop. I then got my first aid kit out and, another horror moment, my kit was not up to scratch at all.

How embarrassing when my client is a nurse.

I stopped it bleeding. Actually being a nurse she did to be fair. I felt physically sick, not because of the blood. I just could not believe what I had done. How careless!!

I then did her waxing and she left.

The feeling would not go away. I messaged her daughter and asked what drink she liked. I knew where she lived and thought I would take her a bottle as an apology. Not much in the grand scheme of my error, but it was a little apology.

I was so angry at myself. You may wonder why. Firstly, I had not trusted my instincts. I knew I was out of sorts and over tired and I should have told my client what was going on.

She was tired too but did not want to let me down. I did not communicate and I was not honest. This is not how I would describe myself and that is why I was angry. I had not been true to me!

The last point is something I always am, I was just really not myself and did not want to start crying but I should have just been more open.

Clients will understand and if they don't, they are not your right client. You would understand if it was the other way around.

Ok, so, I took the bottle. She laughed and said I really shouldn't have. Oh, my goodness, I absolutely should have, and I should have done more too. Not sure what though.

I was talking to her, saying my apologies 100 times, then we noticed there was chaos on the road.

People were out of their cars, up in arms. The whole time I had been stood at my client's door and we hadn't realised.

My client went to see what the commotion was all about.

You guessed it. It was me again!! Oh no this is turning out to be the day from hell and it is barely 11am!! Why????

It turns out my handbrake, although on, had somehow slipped and it was not in gear, and it had rolled down the road and was now at an angle blocking the whole road.

Now there is a silver lining here. There were so many parked cars and somehow my car was unscathed.

Wow!!!

What a miracle. Maybe the day was not so bad.

I was mortified; however, we laugh about it now. This story is way funnier when I act it out or I talk to my client, but I hope you get the gist.

It was one of those moments where I should have put myself first and by doing so, I would have:

- Helped my client who was too tired and over worked.
- I would have not sliced her foot.
- My car would not have blocked the road and angered all the neighbours.
- I would not have been late for my next thing I had to do.
- I would not have arrived to see my Mum feeling absolutely fed up.

And probably so many more things I cannot think of right now. But, if I had either got my lady in on the Wednesday or asked if we could have changed it, none of this would have happened.

It was a real wake up call for me and this made me put lots of changes in place and now I do not work Thursdays at all, nor do I work late on a Wednesday.

I realised these times were just not suiting me anymore.

We must put ourselves first and in turn we can give the best service to our clients and our family and ourselves.

Please think about this.

FINAL TIPS

Remember, Beauty Therapy is a customer facing role, so you will need to be open, friendly and approachable.

As much as the job is about carrying out treatments, I always say it is only 20% of the job.

You are providing a service and your clients are taking time out of their day to spend money on whatever treatment you carry out. You need to make their experience as relaxing and enjoyable as possible. They need to feel incredibly special.

If you have a closed off, distant personality, your client may feel uncomfortable and will perhaps go elsewhere in future.

This industry relies heavily on client loyalty, so make your clients want to come back!

You may be a little shy and nervous at first when you are just starting out but try your best to make your client feel comfortable and relaxed around you and soon you will feel the same.

Most of all, if you are planning on starting out in Beauty, have fun!

It can be a lovely career to get into and it can be so rewarding and so much fun. However, like anything, it is nerve racking at first learning new things, but enjoy it!!

As I mentioned I have sublet, owned properties, sold properties, employed people and sacked people. There are certain aspects of running a business that are not as much fun as just 'doing the job'.

Decide whether it is a business you want, with staff. Is your goal to be hands off and eventually step back from the business. By this I mean what is your 5 or 10 year plan? Do you want to stay working 'in' the business forever?

I now employ staff and train salon owners to have the best work/life balance. This has not been easy for me, as I did not have all of the tools until approximately 5 years ago. If only I knew what I know, now, 20 years ago. However, we cannot dwell on things. Like I said, everything happens for a reason. This is my belief anyway.

I enjoy the training and my skincare and found my passion here now even more than in the treatments.

I understand that so much of what I am saying sounds amazing. But the reality can be completely different.

Business is difficult, but with the right tools and the right people around you it does not have to be.

This is why I have set up my formula for systemising your salon.

Whether you want to stay working in your business as a one-man band or you want a team of people doing the work for you, we need some systemisation.

The business needs to work well for you, your goals and your family life.

You may be wondering what is my formula?

Well funnily enough it is:

S.Y.S.T.E.M.I.S.E

CREATING SALON SUCCESS

To create a smooth running business we need strategies. If you follow the SYSTEMISE formula you can have a balanced life and business. Remember mindset is everything and there is a whole section on it under the YOU section.

Below are some examples of what is involved. There is so much more as well.

S – Systems

When you have systems, your salon can be much easier to manage. When we look at systems it involves things like:

- A manual so that everyone knows how to open up, close up, set up and perform treatments.
- Online booking systems.
- Social media content planning and scheduling

Y – You

All about you and your mindset! However, we need to look after ourselves by looking at:

- Dreams and visions
- Goal setting
- Creating boundaries

S – Sales

Money is a big part of business. It is something we can all feel uncomfortable about. However, we must become comfortable to achieve success. We look at:

- Cash flow
- Pricing structure for profit
- Money mindset
- Selling without selling

T – Time

Managing your time is crucial and one of the least valued commodities. It is so precious and cannot be replenished:

- Time management
- Working less hours
- Finding your why

E – Employee Satisfaction

This is a must, even if you are a one-man band. You are still your employee, even when self-employed. You must see yourself as an employee.

- Keeping staff motivated
- Business vision and mission
- Goal setting

M – Marketing

Marketing your business is a must. It can change the way people see your business and make people come back time and time again, whilst attracting new customers too.

- Having marketing resources
- Creating your business vision and mission statements
- Social media strategies

I – Integrate with like-minded people

This is a must when running a business. It can be a really lonely place and unless people are there doing what you do, they do not understand.

- Why you join networking groups
- Understanding online networking
- How to create your best business pitch

S – Satisfaction of the customer

Customers are the key to our business. We have to keep them happy and provide THE best service possible, whilst keeping our boundaries in place.

- Knowing your customer journey and perfecting it
- The importance of body language
- Wowing your customer every time

E – Efforts to innovate

Making innovations within your business is what will make your business stand out from the rest.

- Learning about membership programmes
- Making yourself an industry expert – writing a great blog
- Importance of some sort of website

Following my SYSTEMISE formula could really help you create a smooth-running Beauty Salon. One that works for you and your lifestyle. If you would like to know more, please get in touch.

Join my group at:
https://www.facebook.com/groups/CreatingSalonSuccess
or have a look at my website www.CreatingSalonSuccess.co.uk

I created a membership group to make coaching accessible for everyone. One to one is available too, of course, but having the support from like-minded people is priceless too.

Thanks so much for taking the time to read this book. I hope you have enjoyed venturing into the crazy life of Louisa and salon world. Equally, I hope you have got some strategies you can use to find out what you truly want out of life and how to create a streamlined business that works for you.

Lots of love and light
Namaste

Louisa x